The Cuisine of Puebla, Cradle of Corn

The Cuisine of Puebla, Cradle of Corn

A Mexican Culinary Journey

Karen Hursh Graber

With illustrations by the author

The Cuisine of Puebla

TABLE OF CONTENTS

Karen Hursh Graber

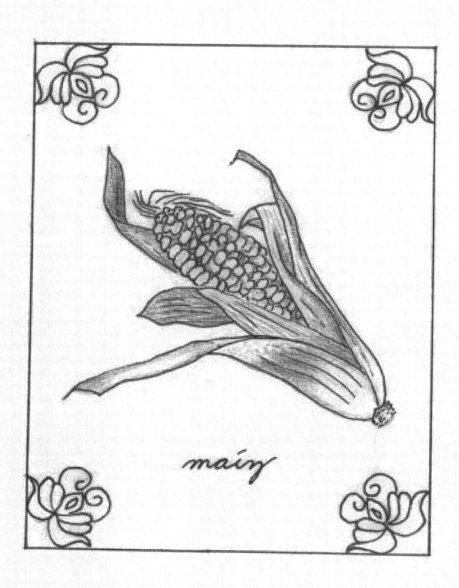

maíz

The Cuisine of Puebla

Introduction

Along an interior wall of the Palacio Municipal in Tehuacan, Puebla, painted in the grand tradition of the great Mexican muralists, marches a cast of characters ranging from pre-Hispanic emperors to heroes of the revolution, all of whom have had a significant impact on the history of this ancient community. There, along with presidents and conquistadors, soldiers and slaves, is archeologist Richard MacNeish, discoverer of the oldest kernels of cultivated corn on earth.

Among the caves and arroyos of this southernmost part of the Valley of Mexico, over twelve thousand years of agricultural history were perfectly preserved. MacNeish's work, begun in 1960, entitled the people of this region to call their land *La Cuña del Maíz* - The Cradle of Corn. This proud title signifies for them not only a strong agricultural heritage, but a time-honored culinary tradition which, with the introduction of the Old World ingredients brought by the Spaniards, has evolved into modern Mexican cuisine.

This creative blending of diverse ingredients is the hallmark of Mexican cooking, and in Puebla it is a passion. Everywhere there is talk of food. People give detailed accounts of what they've just eaten, plan to eat later, or what was served at the most recent *fiesta*. There are over three hundred *moles* in the state of Puebla, with each town or village having its own special version, invariably served at weddings and on holidays. The Poblano enthusiasm for the subject is born of pride in one of the oldest and most savory regional cuisines of Mexico.

Long before the Spaniards came to the area and built the city of Puebla, the nearby town of Cholula was the ceremonial center of the cult of the god Quetzalcoatl, the feathered serpent. As such, it attracted pilgrims from all over what is now Central Mexico and offered, along with incense and flowers, prostitutes and clowns, street food comprised of corn dough in all its guises. The *tamales* and *chalupas* sold to the worshippers who thronged to the great pyramid were essentially the same versions of these foods sold on the streets of Puebla today.

On a corner two blocks from where I live, near the base of the Cholula pyramid, the woman who makes the tortilla-like snacks called *tlacoyos*, patting out the dough with the rhythmic motion that has been called "the heartbeat of Mexico", cannot remember a time when someone in her family did not work at that very spot, in front of a small charcoal burner, doing the same thing. The strength of this thread of tradition was made startlingly clear to me when I found out that their family name is, indeed, Tlacoyo.

Living in a traditional Mexican town has presented a unique opportunity to participate in the *fiestas* that take place throughout the year and the ceremonies which mark the rites of passage throughout a lifetime. My husband and I have been sponsors at a number of family celebrations, and are therefore considered *compadres*, members of the extended family, normally a huge group requiring the preparation of enormous quantities of food for these occasions.

I have always enjoyed helping with these meals, and have learned a great deal not only from friends but from our travels throughout the region. Wherever we go, our interest in the local specialties is met with enthusiasm. I have been invited into restaurant kitchens to learn techniques first-hand, and received patient, detailed explanations on the use of unfamiliar ingredients from the vendors of produce, herbs and spices in the marketplaces.

This book breaks Puebla down into its four distinct culinary regions, each having its particular traditions and special feast days, as well as those it shares with other parts of the state and country. With the Spanish colonial capital city at its center, Puebla reaches north into the Sierra Madre Oriental, with its abundant fruit orchards and mountain streams, and south into the starkly beautiful Oaxacan desert. From the sophisticated recipes which have been handed down in the city of Puebla itself since the days of the viceroys, to the ancient deep-pit barbeque of the rugged southern part of the state, a variety of ingredients and techniques are represented in this part of the country.

I have fond memories of hospitable people and unforgettable food throughout the state of Puebla. Whether we plan in advance to attend a specific local *fiesta*, or just stumble upon one accidentally, our journeys never fail to be interesting. After years of observation and practice under the watchful eyes of my various teachers, I have learned to interpret a "pinch" of this and a "handful" of that, and have tried to make the wonderful recipes of Puebla as accurate, authentic, and accessible as possible.

The recipes are presented by region, followed by an index of recipes listed by course, for easy reference and menu planning.

molcajete

The Cuisine of Puebla

CHAPTER I

Characteristic Ingredients, Techniques and Sources

This is by no means a comprehensive list of the wide variety of ingredients used in Mexican cooking, but a guide to those used in this book. The availability of Mexican herbs, spices and produce north of the border has increased dramatically in recent years. Most of the following items can be found in supermarkets and Latin grocery stores.

Following this section is a list of mail-order and Internet sources for items which may be more difficult to find outside large cities.

Adobo: A paste made of spices and ground chiles, used to flavor meat, poultry and fish.

*Ajonjolí:***Sesame seed** Used toasted and ground in certain *moles* and *pipian*, they are considered indispensable for garnishing *mole poblano.*

*Anís:***Anise** A sweet, aromatic seed used frequently in Poblano cooking, it is one of the requisite ingredients in *mole poblano.*

*Cacahuate:***Peanut** Found in *moles* and *pipian*, sweets and cookies, it is generally ground for use in Mexican cooking, especially in the Sierra of Puebla.

*Canela:***Cinnamon** Used since the time of the Spanish conquest to flavor a variety of sweets and savory meat and poultry dishes, it is almost always sold in sticks and used freshly ground. Mexican cooks use true cinnamon, *cinnamomum zeylanicum*, as opposed to cassia, which is sold as cinnamon in the United States.

Chiles: The fruit of the capsicum plant, chiles were cultivated in the Tehuacan Valley of Puebla beginning at about 7200 B.C. and, along with corn and beans, formed the staple diet of the region. The chiles used in the recipes in this book are listed below.

Fresh Chiles:

Jalapeño: This is a small-to-medium, oval-shaped chile, varying in color from green to dark reddish-green to bright red. Pickled jalapeños, available in cans, are called *jalapeños en escabeche.* Mild to medium hot, it becomes a *chipotle* when dried and smoked. Large jalapeños are called *cuaresmeños* and, in Puebla, *huachinangos.*

Poblano: This large, dark green-to-red triangular-shaped chile is used frequently for stuffing. It varies from mild to medium-hot and, when dried, is called an ancho.

Serrano: A small, bright green chile, it is used in stews, salsas and for pickling. Mild to medium hot, the *serrano* is the chile of choice for uncooked salsas.

Dried Chiles:

Ancho: The mature, dried *poblano* is dark brown and wrinkled, with a mild, fruity flavor. The *ancho* adds color and body to a variety of stews found in the Puebla region.

Arbol: A small, dark red chile, considered very hot and frequently added whole to soups and stews when a piquant flavor is desired.
Chipotle: The dried *jalapeño, chipotle* is cured and smoked, giving it a color ranging from dark reddish-brown to a coffee tone. It is available canned in adobo sauce. The larger varieties are called *chipotle meco* or *chile tamarindo.*

Guajillo: Long, smooth and reddish brown in color, the *guajillo* is considered mild and often used in combination with *anchos* and *pasillas* in Poblano cooking.

Morita: Small, cone-shaped and dark reddish-brown in color, the *morita* has a hot, smokey taste resembling that of the *chipotle*.
Mulato: Similar to the *ancho*, but nearly black in color, it gives a rich, dark color to the *moles* of Puebla.

Pasilla: This is a dried *chilaca*, a long, dark green chile that turns black as it loses moisture. It is not often found fresh in Puebla, where it is nearly always used dried.

*Chocolate Mexicano:***Mexican chocolate** Flavored with almonds and cinnamon, Mexican chocolate is used as both a beverage and in cooking certain *moles*, most notably *mole poblano*. It comes packaged in round tablets, often found in the US under the brand names Ibarra and Abuelita.

*Comino:***Cumin** A strong-smelling seed, with a distinctive flavor, cumin is nearly always toasted whole and then freshly ground in Poblano cooking, and always in quantities much smaller than those used in northern, or Tex-Mex, recipes.

*Crema:***Cream** Mexican cream, sold as *crema natural*, varies in thickness, becoming thicker as it ages. Crème fraîche can be substituted for *crema natural* in sauces and soups. *Crema dulce* is a sweet cream called for in desserts and is the equivalent of American whipping cream, sometimes called heavy cream.

Herbs

The following herbs are found in recipes throughout the book. They are only a few of the astounding number of herbs, both wild and cultivated, that grow in the Puebla region.

*Amaranto:***Amaranth** (*amarantus hypochondriachus*): The seeds of this plant are used to make candy and as a nutritional supplement in milkshakes. In the states of Puebla and Tlaxcala, they are found in a *mole* sauce for chicken. Amaranth seeds are available in health food stores everywhere.

*Cilantro:***Coriander** (*coriandum sativum*): A self-seeding annual with a pungent flavor, cilantro is used in a great variety of Mexican dishes, especially those containing tomatillos, such as green *moles* and salsas.

***Corteza de maguey:*Mixiote** (*agave americana*) The outermost leaf layer of the century plant, it is used to wrap the spiced meat packages called *mixiotes*. This plant is endangered in some areas and the wrapping is replaced in cooking with *papel para mixiotes*

***Epazote:*Wormseed** (*chenopodium ambrosioides*) A hardy perrenial, this herb grows wild in Mexico and many parts of the US. It is unsurpassed in flavoring black beans, quesadillas and many mushroom dishes, and used to treat a variety of stomach ailments.

***Hierba buena:*Spearmint** (*mentha spicata*) This aromatic herb is used in meat stews, cooked sauces and soups. Its leaves are added to cold drinks and used to make tea.

Hierba santa* or *hoja santa (*piper uritum,piper sanctum*) Abundant in south-central Mexico, the palm-sized, anise-scented leaves are used in green *moles* and chicken dishes, as well as for wrapping tamales and fish for steaming.

***Mejorana:*Marjoram** (*origanum onitis*) Along with thyme, it is a traditional herb in the *manojo de hierbas de olor*- handful of fragrant herbs- used to season soups and stews. It is also found in most recipes for marinated vegetables.

***Orégano:*Oregano** (*origanum vulgarae*): This variety of oregano is the one most commonly found in Mexico. It is slightly different in flavor than Mediterranean varieties, and for this reason is found dried in Latin markets and labeled "Mexican oregano."

***Perejil:*Parsley** (*petroselinum crispum*): The flat-leaved variety of parsley is typically added at the very end of cooking soups, stews and green *mole*. It is considered a cleanser and often taken in a blended drink in the morning.

*Tomillo:*Thyme (*thymus vulgaris*): This aromatic herb is one of the classic Mexican *hierbas de olor*- fragrant seasoning herbs. It is found in soups, stews, sauces, marinades and pickled chiles.

*Hoja de aguacate:*Avocado leaf Used fresh or dried, the leaf of the Mexican *criollo* avocado is used in Puebla to season *mixiotes* and to wrap meats for steaming. It may be found dried in Latin markets and is available by mail order.

*Hoja de maíz:*Corn husks These are used both fresh and dried to wrap different types of tamales. The dried husks are widely available in US supermarkets.

*Huitlacoche:*Corn smut The black mushroom that grows on corn during the rainy season in Puebla and other parts of Central Mexico is gaining in popularity in the US, where it is sold canned under the brand name Hérdez. It gives a rich, earthy color and flavor to sauces and is frequently used in quesadillas.

*Manteca:*Lard Rendered pork lard is certainly not for the cholesterol-conscious, although no less an authority on Mexican cooking than Diana Kennedy has stated many times that nothing can take its place. However, if your diet does not permit the use of lard, corn oil is the most acceptable taste substitute and is replacing lard among a growing number of health-conscious Mexicans.

*Masa:*Corn dough The basis of tortillas and their myriad variations, *masa* is made from dried corn kernels which have been soaked in powdered lime (a process called nixtamalization) and cooked until the skins can be rubbed off, at which point it is mixed with water to form a dough. *Masa harina* is a packaged corn dough mix made from nixtamalized corn which is found in the flour section of US supermarkets.

Mixiote: This is the name given to parchment-wrapped bundles of spiced meat, as well as to the wrapping itself. Containing chicken, lamb or beef, they are specialties of the states of Puebla, Tlaxcala and Hidalgo.

Mole: The name given to any of a number of sauces made by combining seeds, herbs, spices or all three. Although *mole poblano* contains chocolate, there are many that do not, and which resemble stews rather than thick sauces. *Mole* is often sold in jars in the Mexican section of US supermarkets, but is markedly inferior to the homemade product.

*Nopales:***Cactus Paddles** Found throughout Mexico and the Southwestern US, they can be boiled, grilled, marinated and used in soups, stews, salads and egg dishes.

*Pepitas:***Pumpkin seeds** Toasted and ground, they are used in *moles*, *pipians*, and other meat and vegetable stews and sauces.

*Piloncillo:***Dark brown sugar** Actually a type of molasses, it comes in cones and is used for both desserts and savory dishes such as pickled *chipotle* chiles. Buy it at a Latin market or use the darkest brown sugar available as a substitute

*Pimienta gorda:***Allspice berry** Growing in abundance in the Sierra of Puebla, allspice is used in sauces, *moles*, *pipians* and as a pickling spice.

Pipian: Similar to its cousin, *mole*, *pipian* is set apart in that it always contains ground seeds, such as pumpkin, sesame and chile seeds, whereas moles often do not.

Platano macho: **Plantain** The Latin American cooking banana is used in Puebla chiefly in the sweet-and-spicy dark *moles* of the southern part of the state.

*Queso:***Cheese** The following cheeses are used in the recipes in this book:
> *Queso añejo:* An aged cheese, a bit on the salty side, and similar to Romano, which may be substituted for it
> *Queso fresco:* Similar to a mild feta, which may be

substituted for it, this cheese has a spongy texture and is crumbled as a garnish on tacos, enchiladas and tostadas.

Queso manchego: A soft cheese used for melting, for which Monterrey Jack can be substituted. Interchangeable with two other soft Mexican cheeses, *chihuahua* and *menonito*

Quesillo: Also called Oaxaca cheese, it is a fresh string cheese.

Setas:Oyster Mushrooms Chewier and more flavorful than button mushrooms, *setas* were once gathered only in the wild, but increasing demand has led to their cultivation. There are many varieties of wild mushrooms in Mexico, including *morillas* (morels) which many claim to be the tastiest in the world.

Tortillas: The flat corn cakes which have been the staple of the Mexican diet since pre-Hispanic times, tortillas are the basis of countless Mexican meals and snacks and today are found packaged nearly all over the world. Wheat tortillas are not typically used in Puebla.

Techniques

Guisar:Stewing By far the most common way of preparing meat, poultry and sauces, this nearly always means cooking the meat separately from the ingredients that go into making a complex sauce such as a *mole* or a *pipian*. This is traditionally done in a *cazuela*, a large clay pot that works very well to hold, and evenly distribute, the heat. One reason for the separate cooking of meat and sauce is that long, slow cooking is required to blend the flavors of the sauce, generally much longer than that needed to cook the meat or poultry. Another consideration is that the individual cook has more control over the texture when the sauce can be thinned with as much or as little broth as desired. The stock resulting from cooking the meat or poultry can be used as soup base, either immediately or frozen for later use.

The other aspect of cooking the meat separately from the sauce ingredients is that the stock can be made with vegetables instead, making several of the recipes in this book easily adaptable for vegetarians.

Moler:Grinding In Mexican cooking terminology, grinding is an all-purpose word that can mean anything from making a liquid puree to mashing ingredients in a mortar and pestle. Since pre-Hispanic times, Mexicans have used a volcanic stone mortar called a *molcajete* for the grinding of chiles, herbs and spices. The blender and food processor have cut down on the use of the *molcajete* and freed women from the dawn-till-dusk hours that were formerly spent in the kitchen.

If you chose not to use a *molcajete*, the important thing to remember is that even when using a blender or food processor, garlic and salt should be ground first. Another factor to bear in mind is texture; if the sauce is a chunky rather than a smooth one, either mince the ingredients finely by hand or pulse the ingredients very briefly. Especially when preparing uncooked salsas, it is important to avoid over processing. In general, an uncooked salsa should have a rougher texture than a cooked sauce.

Tostar:Dry-Roasting This is most commonly done on a *comal*, a round, flat griddle made of clay or metal. Any griddle with a well-seasoned surface will work. This is a quick process, done over high heat, and involving no oil or liquid, so care must be taken not to over-cook the ingredients being roasted.

Dried chiles, which should always be washed and dried thoroughly before roasting, whether or not they are seeded, take only a few minutes on either side at most. They should be roasted just until their fragrance is given forth, and not until there is any noticeable difference in their color. A burned chile will smell bitter and should be discarded.

The commonly used sauce vegetables- tomatoes, onions and garlic- are also often roasted to bring out their flavors. Tomatoes should be roasted until their skins blister, turning them often on the griddle or *comal* with tongs. The skins are either slipped off or left on, according to the recipe and/or individual preference.

Onions should be peeled before roasting and roasted whole, using the tongs to turn them. Onions will turn brown, but should not blacken. (Mexicans use white onions, which have a more intense flavor than the yellow ones, and accounts for the fact that even a recipe for a large quantity of food only contains about half as much onion as a comparable recipe with yellow onions.)

Garlic should be roasted with its skin intact, on a hot *comal* or griddle. When the skin begins to turn brown and pop, the garlic should be removed and the skin peeled. The pulp will have softened and become fragrant.

Tortillas are always baked on a dry griddle or *comal* and, if not fresh, need to be re-heated on one before serving. The tortilla should be heated on one side until it puffs up slightly, turned over, and heated through on the other side. This is especially important with packaged tortillas, which tend to be harder and drier than those from a *tortillería.*

***Freír:*Frying** There are two types of frying: deep frying is done in a skillet or a special type of *comal* with a well in the center which is used only for this purpose. Deep frying is not common in Poblano cooking, with the exception of some street snacks.

Far more common is "soft-frying", or sautéing, called *sofreír*, which is usually done to soften ingredients or bring out their flavor. This is often the case with dried chiles, which are often soft-fried as an alternative, or in addition to, dry roasting.

Tortillas often need to be soft-fried before being covered with sauce or garnished with other ingredients. When preparing enchiladas, it is usually necessary to soften the tortillas by warming them in a little hot oil before dipping them in the enchilada sauce. This is because, unless it is very fresh, a dry tortilla will fall apart in the hot sauce. The oil should be very hot to avoid the tortilla soaking up oil before it becomes warm and pliable. For tostadas, the tortillas need to be fried on both sides until crispy, then drained, before the toppings are added. Deep frying is not necessary to achieve crispness if the oil is hot enough.

***Poner a Sudar:*Sweating** This refers to the technique used to remove the skins from fresh chiles. Normally not done with small chiles, it is nearly always necessary with poblanos, the large, fresh chiles commonly used for stuffing. The chiles are placed directly on a gas flame or under a broiler until charred all over. They should be turned frequently, using tongs, to assure even roasting, taking care not to cook holes through the outside. The chiles are then put in a plastic bag for 10-15 minutes *para que suden*- to "make them sweat." The skins should then be rinsed off in cold water. For stuffing, the chile is sliced lengthwise up one side, and the seed sack carefully removed.

*Desflemar:***Soaking** This refers to soaking for the purpose of removing some of the bite from a fresh chile or even a strong onion, rather than to the process of softening dried chiles in plain hot water. A solution of white vinegar and water, or salt and water, is used to soak the chiles, since both vinegar and salt absorb the heat. This normally requires about an hour and is frequently done with *poblano* chiles before they are stuffed. Smaller, hotter fresh chiles, such as *jalapeños*, may be soaked overnight in a milk bath after being seeded, usually unpeeled.

*Barbacoa:***Barbequing** This bears little or no resemblance to the US cooking technique known as barbequing, but means cooking meat in its own juices, usually wrapped in banana or other aromatic leaves. This is generally done in a deeply-dug pit but can also be prepared indoors in a steamer.

Sources:

J.L. Hudson, Seedsman
P.O. Box 337
La Honda, CA 94064
www.jlhudsonseeds.net
(Mexican herb seeds)

Redwood City Seed Co.
P.O. Box 361
Redwood City, CA 94064
www.ecoseeds.com
(Mexican herbs and vegetables)

On-line Catalogues:

New Mexico Chile Co.
www.nmcchile.com   (Chile and herb plants and seeds)

Davis Plant and Seed Co
www.davisseed.com   (Chile and herb plants and seeds)

MoHotta-MoBetta
www.mohotta.com   (Dried chiles, spices, corn husks and more)

Pacific Island Market
sales@asiamex.com.   (Masa harina, spices and more)

The Spice House
www.thespicehouse.com   (Mexican spices)

cazuela

CHAPTER II

Angelopolis:
Colonial Culinary Capital

The city of Puebla, often referred to as *Angelopolis* because of its full name of Puebla de los Angeles, is a culinary area in its own right. It was here that the native ingredients and the Spanish imports were first combined to make significantly original cross-cultural dishes, regarded as some of the most sophisticated in Mexico. Because the Spaniards chose to build the city in an area surrounded by well-established indigenous settlements, it was instrumental in the formation of a mestizo national cuisine. Many of the dishes which comprise the country's culinary identity, such as *mole poblano* and *chiles en nogada*, had their origins in the city of Puebla. So strongly are these dishes identified with Mexican cooking that stories of their invention have become part of the national folklore.

Several of these food legends center around Puebla's colonial convents. It was the influence of the Spanish nuns, more than any other single factor, which produced the famous, classic *poblano* dishes. Exquisite *moles* and a variety of sweets bordering on the baroque were born in Puebla's grand conventos.

The city had not existed as a community before the arrival of the Spaniards, and it was built with the goal of establishing a "Spanish city" midway between Mexico City and the port of Veracruz. Churches, convents and monasteries were as important as government buildings in creating a Spanish identity in the midst of indigenous villages. The *conventos* were lavishly designed and richly decorated. Many of these four hundred year old buildings, with their Talavera tiles, Moorish arabesques and stone sculptures, still stand today and are open to visitors. Walking through the courtyards, patios and gardens, with their centuries-old orchards planted with seeds from the Old World, one feels a distinct connection to the past. This seems most tangible in the kitchens, with their beautifully tiled surfaces, intricately carved wooden spoons and handmade ceramic cookware. Harmony was important in a room where so much time was spent.

These nuns were the daughters of wealthy vice regal families, who traditionally dedicated one child to the church, and it is evident by the great variety of ingredients at their disposal that money was no object in the creation of exquisite dishes. Spices from the Oriental trade routes, Arabic elements brought to Spain by the Moors, and Spain's own extensive variety of fruits and grains, were all used in combination with indigenous food. Tomatoes, corn, chiles and chocolate were only a few of the local products enthusiastically embraced by the sisters.

For dishes such as *mole* to have been accepted by the colonial populace, they would have to have been seen as fitting for Spanish nobility, and the nuns, with their practical adaptation to local cooking techniques, did a great deal to influence dining habits. After all, they were in charge of preparing banquets for bishops, viceroys and other visiting dignitaries. If a dish was good enough for a bishop, what colonist could possibly say that it wasn't good enough for his own household?

Tortillas and salsas, *moles* and *pipians* soon began appearing on the tables of the families of New Spain. By far the most widely adopted local food was corn. Spanish families who had formerly scorned the native staple soon found themselves eating corn in one form or another with every meal. Today, the city's myriad street stands, market stalls and restaurants of every size, price-range and description, are testimony to Puebla's unique culinary heritage, from the ancestral corn dough to the imaginative colonial creations.

Chalupas Poblanos
Puebla Style Chalupas

The word *chalupa*, of Nahuatl origin, was the name for the canoe-shaped boats used by the Aztecs to navigate the canals of their capital city, Tenochtitlan. Today, the word refers to a *botana* - a snack or appetizer - popular throughout central Mexico, sometimes formed in the shape of a canoe. It is especially prevalent in Puebla, where it is found everywhere, from street stands where *chalupas* are prepared over charcoal fires, to elegant regional restaurants. Poblano-style *chalupas* are smaller than those found elsewhere, and the park along side the Church of San Francisco is famous for its rows of *chalupa* stands, where miniature versions, the size of silver dollars, are sold. After a stroll around the city's colonial plaza, it takes more than one order of these tasty tidbits to satisfy the hunger for a snack. For an appetizer, however, four per person is about right. An order of *chalupas* is always served with both red and green salsa. They are an excellent way to use meat left from a roast, but the meat can be skipped completely, as it is in Puebla on traditionally meatless Fridays.

Ingredients:

> 1/2 cup *manteca* or corn oil
> 24 3"-diameter tortillas, store-bought, or see the recipe on page 68
> 1 recipe Salsa Verde (below)
> 1 recipe Salsa Roja (below)
> 1 1/2 cups cooked, shredded pork, beef or chicken
> 1 1/2 cups crumbled *queso fresco* or mild feta cheese
> 1 medium white onion, finely chopped

In a large frying pan or deep metal *comal*, heat the lard or oil until a few drops of water sizzle and evaporate when sprinkled into the oil. Have several paper towels ready to drain the tortillas as they are removed from the heat.

Place tortillas, as many as will fit, into the pan and turn

them quickly; they will need only 3-4 seconds on each side to "soft-fry"; they should remain pliable, and not become crispy. Drain them very well on the paper towels.

Spoon red salsa onto half of the tortillas, and green salsa onto the remainder. Top with a bit of shredded meat, crumbled cheese and chopped onions.

Serve immediately. Serves 6 as an appetizer.

Salsa de Chipotle
Chipotle Chile Salsa

This salsa can be used on several varieties of *botanas*, as well as being a good, all-purpose table sauce. Although currently popular among north-of-the-border cooks, the grinding of salsas in a *molcajete*, or mortar, seems to be dwindling here in Mexico. A woman who had just moved from New Mexico to the highlands of Chiapas told of giving a *barbacoa* - a deep-pit barbecue - as a means of getting acquainted with the new neighbors. They responded enthusiastically, and the local women offered to bring the tortillas and a variety of salsas. On the day of the barbeque, panic filled the neighborhood when the electricity went out. It seemed that the women, even in this most indigenous part of Mexico, needed their electric blenders to make salsa, and many didn't even own a *molcajete*. Luckily, electricity and good eating were restored before long.

Ingredients:

1 1/2 lbs. tomatoes, roasted peeled, seeded and coarsely chopped
2-3 large cloves garlic, roasted, peeled and coarsely chopped
3-4 dried morita or chipotle chiles (canned chipotles may be used)
2 tablespoons lard or corn oil
Salt to taste

Place the tomatoes, garlic and chiles in a blender and add

just enough water to make grinding possible. If dried chiles are used, soaking in hot water for 20 minutes is necessary before blending; some of the soaking water can be used as the blending liquid.

In a medium-size saucepan, heat the oil over high heat and add the blended chile mixture. When the mixture begins bubbling, lower the heat and cook for 20 minutes. Add salt to taste. (Note: Many *poblana* cooks leave the charred skin on the tomatoes for a smokier flavor.)

Salsa Verde
Green Salsa

The tomatillo, called *tomate verde* in Mexico, is actually related to the gooseberry rather than the tomato. It ranges in color from purple to bright green, and in size from that of a marble (these tiny ones are called *miltomate*) to that of an average tomato. Its papery husk must always be removed, and the sticky substance under the husk rinsed off.

Ingredients:

    1 1/2 lbs. tomatillos
    3-4 fresh serrano chiles (or more, if you like it *picante*)
    2 large cloves garlic, peeled and coarsely chopped
    1 small white onion, peeled and coarsely chopped
    4 tablespoons chopped cilantro

Place the tomatillos and chiles in a saucepan with water to cover, and bring them to a boil. Continue boiling just until the tomatillos have softened a bit. Do not overcook. Place the tomatillos and chiles, with enough of their cooking water to allow the blades to move, in the blender. Add the garlic, onion and cilantro and blend until all ingredients are puréed. More of the cooking liquid can be added if a thinner sauce is desired. Add salt to taste.

Variation 1: *Salsa Verde con Aguacate*: Add a large,

mashed, ripe avocado when blending the other ingredients, along with a bit more liquid. This salsa should have a smoother, creamier consistency than basic *salsa verde*, and is used as a garnish on tacos, *flautas* (thin, fried tacos) and other snacks.

Variation 2: **Salsa Verde Cruda**: This is an uncooked green sauce, usually served as an accompaniment to lamb or organ meat dishes. Using the tomatillos raw makes the sauce a bit tart and excellent for cutting the strong taste of the meat. To make it, using the same ingredients given for basic *salsa verde*, chop the tomatillos coarsely and put them in the blender with the chiles, onion and garlic, and just enough water so that the blades turn. Pulse for a few seconds, add the cilantro, and pulse for a few seconds more. Add salt to taste. Do not over blend; this salsa should have a coarse, chunky texture.

Setas con Epazote
Oyster Mushrooms with Epazote

This versatile recipe may be served as an appetizer, accompanied by a basket of warm, small tortillas, or rolled in crepes and topped with Poblano Cream Sauce (see Index) It may also be used to fill the fried snack called *molotes* (see Index.)

Epazote, a pre-Hispanic herb known in English as wormseed or Mexican tea, has had a resurgence in popularity in recent years and is now widely available in US supermarkets. Indispensible in cooking Mexican-style black beans, *epazote* is unsurpassed in *quesadillas* and many mushroom dishes.

Wild oyster mushrooms, called *setas*, are available in the markets of Puebla and most of Central Mexico during the rainy season, May through October; however, cultivated mushrooms may be used with successful results.

Ingredients:

1 lb. *setas* or other wild mushrooms
2 tablespoons olive oil

3 large cloves garlic, minced
4 scallions, green part included, finely chopped
2-3 serrano chiles, thinly sliced
1/4 cup finely chopped fresh epazote leaves
salt to taste

Wipe the *setas* or other mushrooms with a damp cloth; *setas* should be chopped and other mushrooms sliced.

Heat the oil in a large frying pan and sauté the garlic and scallions, cooking and stirring over medium heat for 4-5 minutes. Add the chiles, mushrooms and *epazote* and continue cooking another 4-5 minutes or until the mushrooms give off their juices. Add salt to taste and serve immediately with warm tortillas. Makes 4 appetizer serving.

Tinga Poblano
Spiced Tomato Stew

The invention of *tinga* has been traced to the nuns of Puebla's Santa Rosa Convent, now open to the public as a museum with a priceless collection of 16th century Talavera tiles covering its walls and ceilings. This versatile dish, with its oriental spices and liberal use of the native American tomato and chile, is a classic example of traditional *poblano* cuisine. Cooked, shredded pork is placed in a *cazuela* - clay pot - with a sauce flavored by the spices and tomatoes, along with smoky chipotles. Simmered until the meat absorbs the flavor of the sauce, *tinga* can be used as a filling for tacos (a good appetizer, served with miniature tortillas) or as a main dish surrounding a white rice mold, garnished with sliced avocado. It is also used to fill *tortas,* the hefty sandwiches made with French rolls, to top tostadas and to fill *molotes* (see Index.) Most recipes call for the addition of chorizo to *tinga,* but some cooks prefer it without the sausage.

Ingredients:

For the meat:

1 pound boneless pork leg

1/2 large onion, stuck with 2 cloves
4 large cloves garlic, peeled
1 bay leaf
salt to taste

For the *tinga*:

8 ounces chorizo, skinned, crumbled, sautéed and drained of fat
1/4 cup lard or corn oil
4 large garlic cloves, peeled and minced
1 large white onion, sliced lengthwise, then across into half-circles
1 1/2 lbs. ripe tomatoes, roasted, peeled and chopped
2 canned chipotle chiles in adobo sauce, coarsely chopped
1/8 teaspoon ground cinnamon
1 whole clove
2 tablespoons cider vinegar
2 tablespoons dark brown sugar

Place the pork in a stockpot with the onion, cloves, garlic, bay leaf, salt and water to cover. Bring to a boil, lower heat, cover and simmer for 1 1/2 hours, or until the meat is cooked through. This may also be done in a pressure cooker, in which case it will take about 20 minutes from the time the pressure regulator is put on. Allow the meat to cool in its broth. When cool enough to handle, remove and shred the meat, and reserve the broth. Shredding is easily accomplished by using two forks to pull at the meat from opposite directions. Cover the meat and set it aside while the sauce is being made.

Heat the oil or lard in a heavy saucepan and sauté the garlic and onion until the onion becomes transparent. Add the chorizo if using, tomatoes and chiles and continue cooking over medium heat 2-3 minutes, or until the tomatoes begins to soften and render their juice. Stir in the spices, vinegar, sugar, salt and pepper. Add one quarter cup of the cooking broth, cover and simmer over low heat for 30 minutes, stirring occasionally. Add the shredded meat and another quarter cup of broth and cook another 15 minutes. Add salt and pepper to taste. The *tinga* should be thick; if you want it thicker, add one half tablespoon cornstarch dissolved in cold water and stir continuously until the sauce thickens. Tinga may be made a day ahead and reheated over a low flame.

Makes 4-6 main dish servings, or twice that many tostadas, tortas, *molotes* or appetizer servings.

Variation: **Tinga Vegetariana**: This is often used as a filling for the *molotes* sold at market stalls and street stands, probably to eliminate the cost of the meat. It is delicious this way, as well as on a tostada, along with beans and shredded lettuce. Simply prepare the sauce as directed above, eliminating the meat and using chicken or vegetable broth instead of the meat broth.

Tostadas de Tinga
Spiced Tomato Tostadas

These are popular in the *fondas*, small neighborhood restaurants which usually stay open well into the night, serving *cena*, the late supper dear to the heart of most dedicated street food *aficionados*. One of the most common uses for *tinga*, these tostadas make great informal party fare. Make the *tinga* a day ahead, reheat it, and set out the ingredients buffet-style.

Ingredients:

> 1 recipe *tinga* or vegetarian *tinga* (see Index)
> 15-18 tostadas (crisp-fried 5"tortillas)
> 2 cups refried beans
> 2-3 cups shredded lettuce
> Sour cream, Mexican crema or crème fraîche, for topping
> Guacamole, for topping

Begin by spreading the tostada with refried beans. Spoon on some *tinga* and, next, shredded lettuce. Top with cream, guacamole, or both. Makes 15-18.

Tacos Arabes
Roasted Meat Tacos

The 1930's brought a migration of people from Lebanon to Mexico. Fleeing political turmoil in their native country, they brought their culinary traditions with them,
including that of cooking meat *gyro*-style, on a vertical spit alongside a wood or gas flame.

Since this is such a portable method of cooking, Lebanese style roast-meat stands began springing up in Central Mexico. A number of Lebanese settled in the city of Puebla and began selling this meat wrapped in large flour tortillas resembling the pita bread of their homeland. Called *tacos arabes*, they are found in various guises in other parts of Mexico, but their origin and popularity remain closely associated with Puebla.

The following method of preparation uses more conventional means of cooking the meat, while capturing the essential flavor of *tacos arabes*. Large, burrito-size flour tortillas are perfect for these tacos. This recipe can also be made ahead and reheated just before serving, accompanied by warm flour tortillas and salsa.

Ingredients:

2 lbs. lean, thinly-sliced pork steaks
8 pasilla chiles
8 guajillo chiles
1/2 large garlic bulb, cloves peeled
3/4 cup distilled white vinegar
1/4 tablespoon cumin seeds
5 whole cloves
1 large white onion, chopped as finely as possible

Trim any outside fat from the pork steaks and set them aside while you make the marinade.

Wash, seed and devein the chiles and put them in a small saucepan with the vinegar. Bring to a boil, lower heat and simmer, covered, until the chiles soften (about 20 minutes.) Allow to cool a bit and then combine with the garlic and seasonings in a *molcajete*, blender or food processor. The resulting mixture should have the consistency of paste; a bit more vinegar may be added to the blender if necessary. Add salt to taste.

Cook the marinating paste on a low flame, stirring constantly, until bubbles begin to form, then remove it from the heat and allow it to cool. Spread it evenly over each pork steak and stack them up one on top of another in a non-reactive bowl to marinate in the refrigerator for at least 5 hours. (This stack is called a *trompo*, or top, because the meat slices are traditionally stacked beginning with the smallest in diameter at the bottom and ending with the widest, so that the stack of meat placed alongside the flame resembles a top.)

Heat a large skillet, adding a bit of vegetable oil if necessary to prevent sticking, and quickly sear each pork steak until brown on the outside, but do not cook through completely at this point. When all have been seared, allow them to cool until they can be handled.

Using a sharp knife, cut the meat into 1/8"-thick strips and return all of it to the skillet along with the chopped onion and sauté until the onion is transparent. Serve immediately or refrigerate for up to 3 days and reheat in an oiled skillet Serves 12-15.

Caldo de Pollo con Hierbabuena
Chicken Soup with Mint

No Puebla *comida* - the main meal of the day, eaten in the afternoon, usually between two and four o'clock - is considered complete without a soup course. Chicken broth is the base for many other soups, and while people in a hurry often resort to powdered consommé mix, a good, home made broth makes any soup far superior.

While *hierba buena* (mint) is used primarily for tea, it is also frequently found in this region in soups and stews, especially those containing chicken. I was skeptical until I tried it one day while making chicken soup with a friend who grew up here in Puebla. Before I had a chance to ask him what he was doing, he ran out to my kitchen garden, plucked a sprig, and popped it into the pot. He told me that his mother (one of the best cooks I know) always put *hierba buena* in her *caldo de pollo*. It tasted delicious, and now I always add a little when making chicken soup.

Ingredients:

> 1 whole chicken (about 3 1/2 lbs.) cut up, breast cut into 4 pieces
> 1 medium onion, stuck with 2 cloves
> 4 large garlic cloves, peeled and cut in half
> 1 bay leaf
> 6-8 black peppercorns
> 2 celery ribs, with leaves
> 1 small bunch *hierba buena* (spearmint)
> 2 carrots, cut in 1"-long chunks
> 2 ears of corn, cut into 4 pieces each
> 2 chayotes, peeled and cut into 1"-long chunks (or use zucchini)
> salt to taste

Put the chicken in a large stockpot with the onion, garlic, bay leaf, peppercorns, celery ribs, carrots, half of the *hierba buena*, salt and water to cover.

Bring this to a boil, lower the heat and simmer for 1- 1 1/2 hours, or until the chicken is tender. Remove the breast pieces first, because they will become rubbery if overcooked.

Remove the soup from the heat and strain it, saving the pieces of chicken and carrots and discarding the other ingredients.

Return the strained broth to the heat, bring to a boil and add the corn and chayote. Lower heat and cook until the vegetables are done.

When the vegetables are tender, return the chicken and carrot pieces to the pot and simmer 5 minutes longer.

Serve the soup in deep bowls, with a piece of chicken, a piece of corn and some of the carrots and chayote; garnish with a sprig of the remaining *hierba buena*.

Serves 6-8 as a light meal, accompanied by salad and warm

bolillos - Mexican crusty rolls - or French bread. To serve as a first course at dinner, cool the chicken and corn, shred the chicken and cut corn from cobs, and return them to the soup.

Sopa Poblana
Corn and Poblano Chile Soup

The *poblano*, a large, fresh green chile often used for stuffing, is nearly always roasted and peeled before using in a recipe. They are named for Puebla, the area where they were first cultivated. This soup, a permanent fixture in most good regional restaurants in the city, is sometimes served adorned with small chunks of cheese and strips of fried corn tortillas

Ingredients:

1/2 stick butter
1 medium white onion, peeled and chopped
2 cloves garlic, peeled and chopped
6 large, fresh poblano chiles, roasted, peeled and seeded
(see Techniques)
1 1/2 quarts chicken broth
1 1/2 tablespoons flour
1 1/4 cups undiluted evaporated milk or half-and-half
1 cup corn kernels, preferably cut fresh from the cob,
cooked until tender
Salt and pepper to taste

Melt half of the butter in a large saucepan and sauté the onion and garlic over medium heat until the onion becomes transparent. Add the chiles and cook another 2 minutes. Transfer to a blender, purée with the broth, and set aside.

Melt the remaining butter in the saucepan, add the flour, stirring constantly with a wire whisk. Cook for 2 minutes and add the puréed mixture. Continue cooking over low flame, stirring constantly, about 5 minutes or until the mixture thickens. Add the evaporated milk but do not allow the soup to boil. Stir in the corn, add salt and pepper to taste.

Garnish with fried tortilla strips and/or cubes of mild cheese (such as Monterrey Jack, Gouda or manchego.) Serves 8.

Arroz Verde Poblano
Poblano Green Rice

The *sopa seca* - "dry soup", meaning rice or pasta - is always served after the soup course as part of the main meal in Mexico.

The use of fresh herbs and *poblano* chiles in this recipe gives the rice a fresh, green color and distinctive taste. Besides being an intriguing alternative to the usual Mexican red rice (sometimes erroneously called "Spanish rice") this dish is a good accompaniment to plain grilled meat or chicken.

Ingredients:

> 1 cup long grain white rice
> 2 tablespoons vegetable oil
> 3 small or two large poblano chiles, roasted, peeled and seeded (see Techniques)
> 2-3 sprigs fresh parsley
> 2-3 sprigs fresh epazote
> 1/2 medium white onion, chopped
> 2 large cloves garlic, peeled and chopped
> 2 1/2 cups chicken or vegetable broth
> 1/2 cup fresh or thawed frozen peas (optional)
> Salt to taste

Soak the rice in hot water to cover for 15 minutes, then rinse it in a strainer under cold running water until the water runs clear. Drain and let dry.

Heat the oil and sauté the rice, stirring to prevent sticking or burning, until golden.

Puree the chiles, onion, garlic and herbs in a blender with 1/2 cup of the broth. Add the purée to the rice and cook, uncovered, until it has been absorbed. Add the remaining broth, cover and simmer over low heat until all the liquid has been absorbed.

Remove from heat and stir in the peas, if using. Stir to fluff, taste for salt, and serve immediately, garnished with avocado slices if desired. Serves 6.

Chiles en Nogada
Stuffed Chiles with Walnut Cream Sauce

This dish is a tribute to Puebla's late summer-early fall harvest season. Ground or chopped meat is seasoned and combined with raisins, nuts and fruit from throughout the state: apples, peaches and pears from the Sierra, roasted poblano chiles and walnuts from the towns in the central part of the state, and pomegranates from the south.

Chiles en nogada, which in its final presentation features the colors of the Mexican flag, is served all over the country during September, *el mes de la patria*, or patriotism month, but never have I tasted any as good as those made in Puebla's home kitchens. Whole families spend days on end preparing mountains of these delicacies for an all-out patriotic feeding frenzy. There are probably as many versions of this dish as there are cooks in Puebla; I have been given recipes with anywhere from ten to forty ingredients. The following is an authentic, uncomplicated version of the Puebla classic.

Ingredients:

For the filling:

1 1/2 lb. boneless pork, cooked and shredded
oil for frying
4 large cloves garlic, peeled and minced
1 medium white onion, chopped fine
1 1/2 lb. roma tomatoes, peeled, seeded and chopped
1 medium apple, peeled and cut into 1/2" pieces
1 medium pear, peeled and cut into 1/2" pieces
1 medium peach, peeled and cut into 1/2"pieces
1 plantain, peeled and cut into 1/2"pieces
1/2 cup raisins, soaked in warm water until softened, then

drained
1/2 cup blanched, slivered almonds
2 ounces candied citron (optional)
1/4 teaspoon ground cinnamon
1 pinch *each*: ground cloves and saffron
salt and pepper to taste
1/3 cup dry sherry

For the chiles:

12 large poblano chiles, roasted and peeled (see
Techniques)
4 eggs, separated, at room temperature
3-4 tablespoons flour
corn oil for frying

For sauce:

2 cups unsweetened heavy cream
2 ounces cream cheese
2 cups walnut meat, soaked in milk to cover (See Note)
1/2 teaspoon sugar (or more, to taste)
1/4 teaspoon cinnamon

For garnish:

2 pomegranates, peeled and separated into seeds
1/2 bunch parsley, trimmed into small sprigs

Have the meat at room temperature. In a large, heavy
saucepan, heat the oil over medium heat, sauté garlic and onion.
Add tomatoes, fruit, raisins, almonds, citron and spices. Cook,
stirring, until the tomato begins to soften, about 5 minutes. Add
meat and sherry. Cook 5 more minutes. Allow the mixture to cool,
and taste for salt and pepper.

After roasting and peeling the chiles, make a lengthwise slit
in each one and carefully remove the seed sack. Hold them under
running water to rinse out any remaining seeds; do not pull at the

veins, since this may tear the chiles. Stuff them with the cooled filling, gently pat them dry with paper towels and lightly coat them with flour. The easiest way to do this is by spreading the flour on a plate and rolling the chiles in it, taking care not to lose any filling. Allow the chiles to sit and dry thoroughly while you prepare the sauce and batter.

To make the sauce, begin by rubbing off the thin skin which covers the walnut segments. Soaking in milk will have loosened them enough to do this fairly easily. Once the skins have been removed, grind the drained walnuts and put them in a blender with the heavy cream, cream cheese, sugar and cinnamon. The consistency is smoother if the sugar is dissolved in a bit of water first. Leave the sauce at room temperature while you fry the chiles. Some cooks add additional sherry to the sauce.

To make the batter, beat the egg whites until they are stiff, then fold in the yolks. Dip each chile into the batter to coat, then immediately into the hot oil. This means that you will have to have the oil heating (but not to the point of smoking) while you coat the chiles. Although this recipe can be doubled, tripled, etc, never use more than four eggs in one batter, or it will become runny. Therefore, if you are serving a number of chiles, you will have to make several batches of fresh batter. Fry the chiles until golden brown on both sides, top with the *nogada* sauce and serve garnished with pomegranate seeds sprinkled over the sauce, and sprigs of parsley to provide the green part of the requisite patriotic colors. Serves 12.

Note: It is most convenient to buy shelled walnut halves; this saves having to shell so many walnuts. Buying small pieces of walnut meat is inadvisable, because they will be nearly impossible to peel.

Mole del Convento de Santa Rosa
Traditional Mole Poblano

Considered the national dish of Mexico, *mole poblano* originated in the colonial era, as a version of the medieval Spanish court banquet recipes, in which sauces were based on meat broths flavored with spices from the Orient. The significant difference with *mole* was, of course, the combination of these spices with New World ingredients: chiles, tomatoes, tortillas and, most importantly, the turkey. So prized was this creature by the indigenous people that they had no less than forty different words for it, the most widely used in Puebla today being the Nahuatl *guajolote*. The Spaniards later introduced the word *pavo*.

Although there are several versions of the story of its creation, the most popularly accepted tale credits Sister Andrea de la Asunción, of Puebla's Santa Rosa convent, with the original *mole* recipe. Famous among clergy and *poblano* society for her elegant dishes, Sister Andrea was chosen by the bishop to prepare a meal for the Viceroy of New Spain on the occasion of his visit to Puebla on the third Sunday before Lent in 1680. To prepare for this pre-Lenten banquet, Sister Andrea began fattening up a turkey by feeding it chestnuts and hazelnuts to enrich the flavor of the broth which is the base of *mole*.

Although the word itself is of Nahuatl origin, derived from *mulli*, meaning potage or sauce, *mole poblano*, like many other artistic *poblano* creations, is distinctly baroque. Its long-standing popularity makes it indispensable at wedding *fiestas*. Among traditional families here in Cholula, a live turkey is present at the reception. This placid creature is passed from dancer to dancer, absorbing the good feeling of the party, and is cooked the next day for the newlyweds' first *mole*. The first time we attended one of these affairs, my husband attempted a Texas two-step with the unprotesting bird and had to be gently reminded that the *guajalote* did have to last out the wedding.

The *Festival del Mole Poblano*, during which, in addition to the *mole* competition, traditional Poblano table settings are judged, is held for three consecutive Sundays each July. The smells, tastes and sights of the festival are recommended to the visitor who wants to experience an authentic Mexican culinary event.

Ingredients:

For the turkey:

1 8-lb. turkey or two large chickens, cut in serving pieces
2 large cloves garlic, peeled
1/2 white onion, stuck with 2 cloves
1 large bay leaf
water to cover: about 8 cups
salt to taste

For the sauce:

4 tablespoons lard or corn oil
4 ancho chiles, seeded and deveined
6 mulato chiles, seeded and deveined
4 pasilla chiles, seeded and deveined
2 canned chipotle chiles in adobo sauce
2 corn tortillas, torn into pieces
1 medium white onion, chopped
2 large cloves garlic, peeled and coarsely chopped
4 Roma tomatoes, roasted, peeled, seeded and chopped
3 ounces blanched almonds
1 1/2 ounces unshelled, peeled peanuts
4 whole cloves
4 whole allspice
1 1/2" stick cinnamon
1/4 teaspoon aniseed
1/4 cup lightly toasted sesame seeds
2 ounces raisins
2 ounces Mexican chocolate (1 tablet)

1 teaspoon sugar
Salt to taste

Place the turkey or chickens in a stockpot with the garlic, onion, bay leaf, water to cover and salt to taste. Bring to a boil, then lower flame, cover and simmer until tender. Remove from heat, let the turkey or chicken cool in the stock, then strain, reserving the stock, and set aside.

In a large, heavy saucepan or Mexican *cazuela*, heat one tablespoon of the lard or oil and briefly sauté the ancho, mulato and pasilla chiles for two minutes, stirring constantly. Take care not to burn them; they should be sautéed only to the point of fragrance. Put them in a bowl with enough of the broth to cover, and soak for twenty minutes. Puree them in a blender, along with their broth and the chipotles, remove and set aside.

Heat another tablespoon of lard or oil in the same saucepan and fry the tortilla pieces, onion, garlic and tomatoes for three minutes. Transfer them to the blender with just enough broth so that the blades will turn; puree, remove and set aside.

Heat a third tablespoon of lard or oil, add the almonds, peanuts, spices and half the sesame seeds and sauté for two to three minutes more. Transfer to the blender, add the raisins and broth to cover, and puree.

Heat the remaining tablespoon of lard or oil in the same large pot or *cazuela* and add all the pureed ingredients, mixing thoroughly. Boil for five minutes over medium heat, stirring constantly. Add the chocolate and sugar and keep stirring until the chocolate melts. At this point, the *mole* will have the texture of a loose paste. Add enough broth (about two cups) to give the sauce the consistency of heavy cream. Simmer it, covered, over low heat, for about twenty minutes, stirring from time to time. Add salt to taste, and more stock if the sauce is too thick.

Add the turkey or chicken pieces, cover and continue cooking for ten more minutes. Serve the *mole* in bowls, with the remaining sesame seeds sprinkled on top, accompanied by warm corn tortillas. Mole freezes well, and may be reheated over low heat in a heavy saucepan. It can be used to fill tamales or as a sauce for enchiladas. Serves 8-10.

Note: Mexican chocolate is widely available in the US, with Ibarra being a popular brand for use in *mole poblano*. Two ounces are about equivalent to one of the round, individually-wrapped pieces that come six to a box.

Manchamanteles Poblanos
Chicken and Fruit Stew

The name *manchamanteles* literally means "tablecloth stainers", because of the spots that can result from dripping any of the deep red sauce. In Puebla this dish usually contains both chicken and pork, not an unusual combination in Mexican cooking. It can be made with chicken alone, but the *plátanos machos*- plantains, or Latin American cooking bananas- are requisite, along with the sweet potatoes. Fruit varies from season to season and region to region.

Ingredients:

For the meat:

2 lbs. pork loin plus 4 chicken breasts OR 2 chickens, cut into serving pieces
1 medium white onion, studded with two cloves
6 carrots, peeled and cut into chunks
6 large cloves garlic, peeled
2-3 sprigs each thyme and marjoram
salt to taste
water to cover

For the sauce:

2 tablespoons lard or oil
8 ancho chiles, seeded and deveined
2 ounces blanched almonds
1 1/2" stick cinnamon
4- 6 Roma tomatoes, roasted, peeled, seeded and chopped
1 small white onion, sliced

2 large garlic cloves, peeled
2 plantains, peeled and sliced
2 yellow sweet potatoes, peeled and sliced
3 thick slices fresh, sweet pineapple, cut into chunks
1 small apple, peeled and cut into chunks (optional)
1 small pear, peeled and cut into chunks (optional)
1 1/2 teaspoons sugar
salt to taste

Put the cut-up chickens or the pork loin in one piece together with the chicken breasts cut into fourths, in a stockpot with the onion, carrots, garlic, herbs, salt to taste and water to cover. Bring to a boil, lower heat and cook, covered, until tender. This will take approximately one hour for the dark meat of chicken and the pork, and about half that time for white meat of chicken, so whether you are using both meats or chicken only, the breast pieces must be removed first. Allow the chicken and meat to cool in the broth, strain the broth and reserve. If using chicken only, cover the pieces and set aside. If using a chicken-pork combination, thinly slice the pork and skin, bone and shred the chicken; cover and set aside.

Heat one tablespoon of the lard or oil in a large, heavy saucepan or *cazuela* and sauté the chiles for two minutes, stirring constantly, just until their fragrance is released; take care not to burn them, since this results in a bitter flavor. Put them in a bowl with broth to cover for twenty minutes.

Add another half tablespoon of lard or oil to that remaining in the saucepan in which the chiles were sautéed, and fry the almonds, cinnamon, cloves, tomatoes, onion and garlic until the tomato just begins to release its juice. Put this mixture in a blender with the chiles and the broth in which they were soaked, and puree till smooth, using the highest setting.

Heat the remaining half tablespoon of lard or oil in the same saucepan or *cazuela* and pour all of the blended ingredients into the saucepan through a large, wire mesh strainer. Use a spoon to push through as much of the sauce as possible. Cook, stirring, for ten minutes, gradually adding about four cups of broth. Add the plantains, sweet potatoes, fruit, sugar and salt to taste and continue cooking, covered, on low heat for another twenty minutes. Add the cooked chicken and pork and heat through. Serve in bowls, accompanied by white rice and warm tortillas. Serves 8-10.

Rompope de Santa Clara
Mexican Eggnog

After long hours spent on complicated recipes, the nuns evidently treated themselves to a little something warm inside those cold *convento* walls. From the Santa Clara Convent came *rompope*, a beverage resembling eggnog but, unlike eggnog, never sold bottled as a nonalcoholic beverage. In Mexico, bottled *rompope* has about the same alcohol content as beer; however home made versions vary in their alcohol content. The original recipe called for cane alcohol; this one uses the optional addition of light rum. *Rompope* is an ingredient in several delicious desserts, a variety of which follow.

Ingredients:

    1 1/2 quarts of milk
    1/2 cup almonds, peeled and ground to a paste
    1 1/2 cups sugar
    1 stick cinnamon
    1/2 teaspoon nutmeg
    2 whole cloves
    8 egg yolks
    white rum to taste (optional)

Heat the milk in a saucepan over medium heat until bubbles form around the edge of the pan. Add all remaining ingredients except the egg yolks and rum, and cook at a low boil, stirring continuously, until the mixture thickens to the consistency of half-and-half. Remove it from the heat and let it cool to room temperature.

Beat the egg yolks; return the milk mixture to medium heat and slowly add the beaten egg yolks, stirring continuously with a wire whip until they are all incorporated.

Remove the *rompope* from the heat, let it cool once again, and add white rum to taste. Serve alone as a holiday beverage, or in one of the following recipes.

Mousse de Rompope
Rompope Mousse

This is an interesting and delicious change from the usual chocolate mousse, and a perfect dessert after a big meal, Mexican or otherwise.

Ingredients:

> 4 envelopes unflavored gelatin
> 1 cup cold water
> 3 cups evaporated milk
> 1 can condensed milk
> 1 1/2 cups rompope (above, or use bottled rompope)
> 3 eggs, separated

Dissolve the gelatin in the water and set aside. Mix both kinds of milk with the beaten egg yolks in a medium saucepan. Bring it to a boil over low heat and allow it to boil one minute without stirring. Meanwhile, beat the egg whites until stiff peaks form.

Mix the dissolved gelatin into the milk and fold in the egg whites. Fill a mold with the mousse and chill thoroughly. Unmold just before serving and decorate with sliced strawberries, kiwis, or the fruit of your choice. Serves 8.

Fresas al Rompope
Strawberries with Rompope Cream

Fresas con crema - strawberries with cream- is a popular dessert in Central Mexico. This variation uses rompope to flavor the whipped cream.

Ingredients:

> 3 cups sliced strawberries
> 1/2 cup granulated sugar
> 1 cup whipping cream
> 1/4 cup rompope (p.27, or use bottled rompope)
> 1/2 cup confectioners' sugar

Mix the sliced strawberries in a bowl with the granulated sugar and refrigerate for one hour.

Whip the cream until stiff peaks form, and mix in the rompope and confectioners' sugar. Fold this mixture into the strawberries and serve in dessert glasses, decorated with whole strawberries and mint leaves if you wish. Serves 6.

Arroz con Leche
Mexican Rice Pudding

Although popular all over Mexico, this dessert originated in Puebla. The recipe was given to me by Doña Lucia, proprietor of Las Cazuelas de Cholula, specializing in home made mole pastes and spices. I love the smell of her booth, especially the cinnamon sticks. If true stick cinnamon (*cinnamomum zeylanicum*) is unavailable, use ground cinnamon instead, substituting 1/2 teaspoon for a 2"piece of cinnamon stick.

Ingredients:

> 1 cup long grain rice
> 2 cups water
> 4 cups milk
> 3/4 cup sugar
> 1/4 teaspoon salt
> zest of 1 lime, cut into thin strips
> 1 2" piece of cinnamon stick
> 2 ounces raisins, soaked until soft, then drained

Soak the rice in hot water to cover for 15 minutes, rinse in a colander under cold water until the water runs clear and let the rice dry.

In a heavy saucepan, bring the 2 cups water to a boil, add the rice, cover and cook over low heat until the water is absorbed. Add the milk, sugar, salt, lime zest, cinnamon and raisins. Mix well to blend ingredients, cover and cook over low heat until the milk is absorbed and the rice is creamy. Serve warm or cool, dusted with ground cinnamon. Serves 8.

Pastel de Almendras
Layered Almond Cake

This cake, in one version or another, has been around since the Spaniards brought almonds to the Americas. This was not considered an indulgence, since sugar-coated almonds were said to be good for the sick. This dessert is best if made a day in advance, so that the cake layers absorb the full flavor of the sherry and the almond icing.

Ingredients:

4 eggs, separated
1 cup sugar
1 cup sifted flour
1/8 teaspoon salt
1 1/2 teaspoons baking powder
1/2 teaspoon grated lime zest
1 teaspoon vanilla

For the sherry syrup:

2/3 cup sugar
1/2 cup water
1/2 cup sweet sherry

For the almond icing:

2/3 cup sugar

2/3 cup water
3 egg yolks
1/2 teaspoon almond extract
1/2 cup slivered, blanched almonds

Beat the egg yolks until fluffy with a wire whip or electric mixer; continue beating, adding 1 cup of the sugar a little at a time. Sift the flour together with the salt and baking powder, and add these ingredients gradually to the egg mixture. Stir in the lime zest and vanilla. Beat the egg whites until stiff and fold them into the cake mixture.

Bake in two greased 9" round layer cake pans at 350° for 45 minutes. Let cool, turn out of pans, and cut each layer in half horizontally.

Make the syrup by combining the sugar, water and half the sherry in a medium saucepan; cook, stirring, for 5 minutes, remove from heat, and stir in remaining sherry. Brush the syrup evenly over each of the layers.

To make the icing, combine everything but the almonds in a medium saucepan and cook, stirring constantly, over low heat for 8-10 minutes, or until the egg thickens. Remove from heat and stir in almonds. Spread the icing evenly over each of the layers as the layers are placed upon one another. Cover and store in refrigerator for one day; bring to room temperature before serving. Serves 8.

Cocada
Coconut Dessert

Although grown in the neighboring state of Veracruz, coconuts are a staple of Puebla's many street stands selling cut-up fruit, usually dressed with powdered chile and lime juice and served in plastic bags, with wooden picks for spearing.

Coconuts found their way into the colonial dessert repertoire, in the form of *cocada*, a confection with the texture of soft fudge. This dessert is best served cold, so plan on making it at least a couple of hours ahead of serving time. Packaged shredded or flaked coconut can be substituted for fresh, but use 1/3 more for every cup. If using fresh coconut, use the coconut liquid instead of water.

Ingredients:

> 1 cup plus 2 tablespoons sugar
> 1 cup cold water or fresh coconut liquid
> 2 tablespoons butter
> 1 cup fresh shredded coconut, or 1 1/3 cups packaged
> 4 lightly beaten egg yolks
> 1/2 stick cinnamon or 1/4 teaspoon ground cinnamon
> 1/2 cup blanched, slivered almonds

In a medium sized, heavy saucepan, combine one cup of the sugar and water or coconut liquid, bring to a boil and cook over medium heat for 10 minutes, stirring constantly, to make a syrup.

Add the butter and the coconut and cook at a slow boil for 15 minutes, stirring often. Remove from heat and stir in the beaten egg yolks and cinnamon, a little at a time.

Return the pan to the heat and cook over high heat, stirring continuously, for approximately 20 minutes or until the bottom of the pan can be seen. Remove from heat.

Pour mixture into a buttered 8" baking dish and sprinkle the remaining 2 tablespoons of sugar and the almonds over the top. Bake in a 325° oven until the top is golden brown. Allow to cool at room temperature. Serve cold. Spooning or slicing the *cocada* on to dessert dishes. Serves 6.

Dulce de Limón
Candied Limes with Coconut Filling

Particularly attractive are the very old, ornate sweet shops found in the *Centro Historico*, the colonial center of the city of Puebla. Often adorned with Talavera tile and lovely hand-painted designs on walls and ceilings, their window displays are artfully arranged and always tempting. Some of the most attractive elements of these displays are the many kinds of candied fruits, shining like colored glass ornaments. This recipe is easy to prepare, especially for such a visually appealing confection. To give these sweets as a gift, tuck a few of them in a small basket lined with an attractive napkin. Or pass them on a tray or candy dish after dinner.

Ingredients:

For the limes:

12 limes, just barely grated (this releases oils from the rind cells)
cold water to cover
1 1/2 cups water
1 1/2 cups sugar
a few drops of green food coloring (optional)

For the coconut filling:

1 1/2 cups water
1 1/2 cups sugar
pinch of salt
1 cup shredded coconut (moist canned coconut can be
        used)
2 tablespoons butter

Cut the limes crosswise at the stem end and scoop out the pulp. Place them in a heavy pan with cold water to cover, and bring it slowly to the boiling point. Simmer for 20 minutes, drain, and repeat the process four more times.

Combine the 1 1/2 cups water and the sugar in a saucepan, bring the mixture to a slow boil, cover and cook for 30 minutes, forming a thick syrup. At this point, a drop or two of the food coloring may be added, since some of the fruit's color is lost in boiling. Add the limes and continue boiling until all syrup is absorbed. Remove the limes from the saucepan, and put them on a rack to dry.

To make the filling, mix the water, sugar and salt in a saucepan, and stir over medium heat until the sugar has dissolved. Bring the mixture to a boil and cook it, covered, over medium heat until the steam has washed down any sugar crystals that may have formed on the sides of the pan.

Uncover and cook the syrup to the soft-ball stage (234° on a candy thermometer, or when a small quantity of the syrup, dropped into cold water, forms a ball which does not disintegrate.) Remove the syrup from the heat and stir in the coconut and the butter. When cool fill the limes with the mixture and place them on trays for the centers to dry. If not serving immediately, store, covered, in a cool place. Makes one dozen.

Camotes
Sweet Potato Candy

White, yellow and purple sweet potatoes are all found in Puebla's markets, and used so frequently in desserts and candies that the same word is used for both the vegetable and the candy made from it. At the entrance to the Puebla-Mexico City highway, dozens of *camote* vendors, with boxes of these popular treats stacked precariously on one arm, use the other arm to flag down cars and thrust their wares toward the drivers, lest anyone leave the city without one of its most popular sweets.

Ingredients:

    4 cups sugar
    1 1/2 tablespoons white corn syrup
    1 cup pineapple juice or water
    2 lbs. sweet potatoes, peeled, cooked and pureed

In a medium saucepan, combine 3 cups of the sugar, the corn syrup and one cup of pineapple juice or water, stirring until the sugar is thoroughly dissolved. Bring the mixture to a boil over low heat; when it comes to a boil, cover it so that the steam will wash down any sugar crystals that form on the sides of the pan. Cook the syrup for 3 minutes, then uncover and cook the syrup until it reaches the "thread" stage, 230° on a candy thermometer, or when the syrup makes a coarse, 2" thread when dropped from a spoon.

Add the sweet potatoes and continue cooking, stirring frequently, until the bottom of the pan can be seen. Remove from heat, beat for one minute with a wire whip, and allow to cool, preferably for a day.

Form the *camotes* into desired shape (the most common looks like a short, fat cigar) and place them on waxed paper in a warm, dry place for one day. (In Puebla, the *camotes* are traditionally dried in the sun.)

Prepare a syrup by combining the remaining cup of sugar with 1/2 cup water in a heavy saucepan, and cooking on medium heat, stirring, until a candy thermometer registers 234°, the "soft ball" stage, at which a small quantity of syrup dropped into cold water forms a ball which does not disintegrate and which flattens out on its own when picked up with the fingers.

Brush the *camotes* with the syrup and place them on waxes paper to dry completely. They should be wrapped in waxed paper and stored in a box or tin, whether for gift-giving or passing around to guests. Makes about 20 candies.

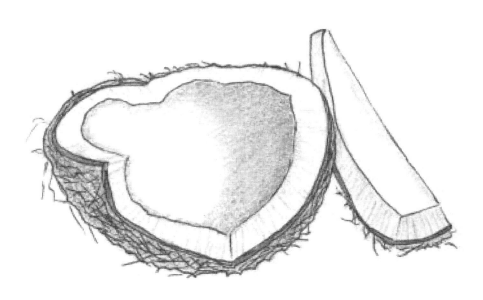

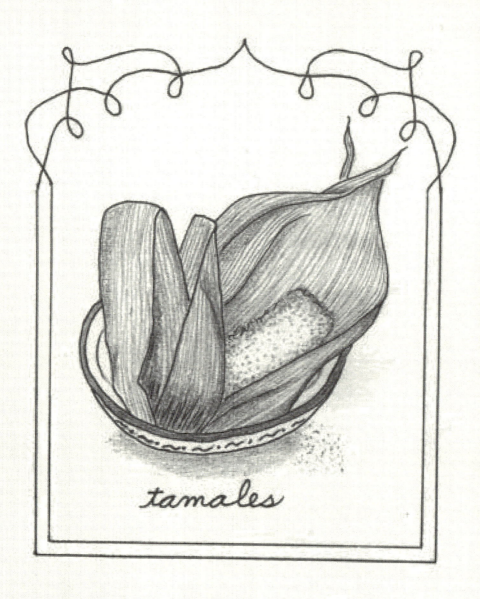

tamales

The Cuisine of Puebla

CHAPTER III

El Centro:
From *Milpa* to Market

The central part of the state, consisting of the towns and villages surrounding the capital, lies along the skirts of two impressive volcanoes. Popocatepetl, or "Smoking Man" in Nahuatl, can be seen from nearly every *pueblo* throughout the central region, as can Popo's "mate", Iztacihuatl, "Sleeping Woman." On their slopes, and further down in the valley, farmers cultivate their *milpas*, the cornfields which even those who work in the city return home to till during the summer rainy season.

In addition to corn and beans which provide the staple diet, a wide variety of other vegetables are grown in this part of the state. Because of this, the area is characterized by its many large markets and twice-weekly *tianguis*- outdoor markets where indigenous women from the smallest villages spread their wares on tarps and blankets, stacking them into artful arrangements of chiles, vegetables, herbs and spices.

While the *milpa* is the man's domain, the market is the woman's. Some markets, such as the centuries-old Cholula market, a hub of activity since pre-Hispanic times, are strictly matriarchal. This means that a market stall cannot be handed down to a male member of the family, but must pass to a female relative, no matter how distant.

Whether brought in by truck or carried on the back in bundles strapped to the head with a tump line, the produce is fresh and attractive. A large part of it is also organic, since only produce grown for export requires chemical treatment for entry into the United States and other countries.

Besides the fruits and vegetables, herbs and spices, there is a wide variety of meat and dairy products. In the late 1800's, a small group of Northern Italian dairy farmers was sponsored by the Mexican government for immigration, settling in the center of the state of Puebla and founding the unique Italian-Mexican town of Chipilo. Their butter and cheese-making techniques helped boost local quality and production, and today excellent cheeses and rich, fresh fruit flavored yoghurts are found in markets throughout the region.

The sights, smells, sounds and tastes of the markets are unforgettable, and so are the people who give it life. From *la pollera*, whose rows of freshly-plucked chickens are lined up neatly on a beautifully embroidered tablecloth, to *el hierbero*, who prescribes herbal remedies from a perch surrounded by bundles of medicinal plants, candles and amulets, each vendor is an expert of a sort. Competition for customers is heavy, and advice is freely given to the customer who chooses to buy from a particular stall.

Market days are among my favorites, and I enjoy going to other towns in the area to check out what might be new to me, or found only at certain times of the year. I am rarely disappointed. Once, in early February, a market was filled with people selling huge piles of fresh rosemary. Thinking that perhaps it was used in the preparation of a seasonal dish, I asked and was informed that rosemary bought and blessed in church on Candlemas Day was kept until the rainy season, when it was burned on the patio as protection against damage or injury from the heavy summer storms.

Each of the markets also has its own version of "restaurant row", with clay *cazuelas* bubbling over charcoal fires and emitting enticing aromas. The women who prepare these tempting dishes, as well as those who sell the various ingredients, have been open, warm and generous in dispensing their culinary counsel. This section contains many of the recipes and techniques they have shared with me.

The Cuisine of Puebla

Tamales
Tamales

Several years ago, not long after arriving in Mexico, we had a neighbor who, although quiet most of the time, would play music at top volume in the very early hours of the morning on Saturdays and Sundays. We wondered about it until we found out that the *señora* sold tamales on weekends, and were told that music is necessary for successful results. Without some form of music, humming or singing going on while they are being made, tamales will not be light, as they should be, but as heavy as silence. If this is true, then our neighbor's tamales, judging from the rousing level of her music, must have been the best in town.

In pre-Hispanic times, tamales were prepared with a variety of herbs, chiles and seeds to flavor the corn dough. They had a special place at the banquets and feast days of the Aztecs and other people of the central highlands, and were stuffed with a particular filling for the festival of each important god - beans for the jaguar god Tezcatlipoca, shrimp and chiles for the fire god Huehueteotl.

Today, tamales are found in a variety of shapes and sizes, with a diversity of fillings from meat, fish and fowl to raisins, coconut and pineapples. They are wrapped in either corn husks or banana leaves, depending upon the region. In central Puebla, they are nearly always wrapped in corn husks and eaten as the first meal of the day. The early morning hours find people gathered around the huge, steaming pots of tamales which are found on street corners in even the smallest *pueblo*, rubbing their hands together, perhaps to ward off the morning chill, or maybe in anticipation of the first tasty bite, but probably a little of both.

The tamal vendors always sell hot drinks of *atole* and champurrado (see Index for these recipes), the beverages of choice to accompany tamales. The basic recipe for tamales using masa harina mix is given below, followed by a variety of fillings used in this region. Experiment with your own fillings; leftover meat, shredded and seasoned, as well as cheese, beans, mushrooms and mole sauces are all good in tamales. For *tamales de mole*, make a filling by mixing one cup of *mole polio* sauce (Chapter I) with one cup of cooked, shredded chicken.

Ingredients:

> 24 dried corn husks, plus extra for lining the steamer
> 1 cup lard
> 2 teaspoons salt
> 1 teaspoon baking powder
> 2 1/2 cups masa harina mix
> 1 1/2 cups water or broth
> 1 1/2-2 cups filling (below)

Place the corn husks in warm water to cover and soak them overnight. Remove them from the water, drain and pat them dry.

Beat the lard, by hand or with an electric mixer, until it is light and fluffy; it should have the consistency of frosting.

In a large bowl, mix the masa harina mix, salt, and baking powder. Add the water a little at a time, beating after each addition to form a light dough.

Add beaten lard to the dough, a little at a time, beating after each addition so that the dough is light and fluffy. To test whether the dough is light enough, pinch off a small piece and drop it in a glass of chilled water. If it floats, it is light enough; if not, continue beating.

To assemble the tamales, trim the corn husks if they have not been trimmed, by cutting off the pointed ends. Lay two corn husks side by side lengthwise so that they overlap by about an inch. Spread 2 tablespoons of dough down the center of the husks, leaving the top, bottom and sides bare. Spoon 1 tablespoon of filling down the center of the dough. Fold the two long sides inward, covering the dough and filling; the bottom and top are then folded toward the center, forming a little package. The ends should be secured by tying a piece of string or a strip of corn husk around the tamal. The procedure is essentially the same as wrapping gift paper around a box.

To steam the tamales, place a rack over boiling water in a steamer or Dutch oven. Many cooks place a coin in the water so that the rattling of the coin will warn them that the water has evaporated. If the water does evaporate before the end of the cooking process, add boiling water, never cold water. Line the bottom of the steamer with corn husks and stack the tamales loosely, allowing room for the dough to expand. Cover with another layer of corn husks and a clean cloth. This is to absorb the moisture that will drip off the lid during the steaming process, and prevent the tamales from becoming soggy.

The steaming will take from 1-2 hours, depending on the altitude and the consistency of the dough. To test for doneness, remove one tamal, untie and open the husks. The tamal is done when the husk comes away easily and the tamal is firm. Serve immediately or refrigerate for up to a week and reheat in the oven. Tamales may also be frozen, packed in freezer bags, and defrosted as needed. Makes 24.

Relleno Rojo de Puerco
Pork and Tomato Sauce Filling for Tamales

In the central Puebla town of Huaquechula, in pastoral countryside far removed from city life, there is an old monastery reputed to have been the place where renegade Franciscans were sent as punishment during the 1500's. The eerie gothic murals that can still be seen inside give credence to the story. Climbing up narrow, winding stairs to the bell tower, after having passed the four hundred year old crypt, it seemed logical when the groundskeeper informed us that Day of the Dead is the town's festival day. The intricately cut paper and clay ceremonial pieces that adorn Day of the Dead altars are made here. Since tamales are considered an indispensable offering to the spirits of the departed, it is not surprising that they are the local specialty. In addition to the tamales meant for the *muertos*, a variety of tamales are made each day. The *tamales rojos*, or red tamales, are those filled with a tomato sauce, which usually contains pork; however, chicken may be substituted.

Ingredients:
    4 roma tomatoes
    2 large garlic cloves

1/2 medium white onion
1 teaspoon salt
1 tablespoon lard or corn oil
4-5 jalapeños, seeded and cut into strips
1/2 lb. cooked pork, shredded or cut into small chunks
(about 2 cups)

Roast the tomatoes and garlic on a hot griddle or *comal* until the tomato skins blister and the garlic skins turn brown. Place unpeeled tomatoes, peeled garlic and the onion in a blender with the salt and enough water or broth to allow the blades to move; blend until a smooth puree is formed.

Heat lard or corn oil in a medium saucepan and add the pureed mixture. Cook over medium heat 10 minutes, add the cooked pork and cook another 10 minutes, or until the sauce is thick. When filling the tamales, place a jalapeño strip in each one before rolling. Makes enough filling for 24 tamales.

Relleno Verde de Pollo
Chicken and Tomatillo Sauce Filling for Tamales

Another form of offering tamales is favored by the people of the *pueblos* closest to the volcano Popocatepetl. When the volcano reawakened in the early 1990's, after nearly one hundred years of inactivity, the villagers, rather than relying on the predictions of scientists, did what their ancestors had always done. They brought offerings of flowers, mole and tamales to appease the spirit of the volcano, familiarly called "Gregorio" by the people who have lived on its slopes for generations. These *tamales verdes* have a mild green sauce filling which may be made more *picante* by the addition of roasted poblano chile strips.

Ingredients:

1/2 lb. tomatillos, husked
1 medium white onion, peeled
2 large cloves garlic, peeled
3 sprigs cilantro

1 teaspoon salt
1 tablespoon lard or corn oil
2 cups shredded, cooked chicken

Place the tomatillos, onion and garlic in a medium saucepan with water to cover. Bring to a boil, lower heat and simmer until the tomatillos are soft. Place the tomatillos, onion and garlic in a blender with the salt, cilantro and enough of the cooking water to allow the blades to move; puree until smooth.

Heat the lard or oil in a medium saucepan, add the tomatillo mixture. Cook over medium heat for 10 minutes, add the chicken and continue cooking for another 5 minutes, or until the sauce has thickened. A strip of poblano chiles may be added to each tamal if desired. Makes enough filling for 24 tamales.

Tamales Dulces:
Sweet Tamales

These are frequently served at children's birthday parties, saints' days of young and old, and for a late supper with a cup of hot chocolate, *atole* (Chapter III))or *champurrado* (below.) The steam whistle of the tamales vendor can often be heard as he walks past with his pushcart, calling "tamal-e-e-e-s" in the nasal twang which distinguishes the street vendor.

Ingredients:

2 bunches dried corn husks
1 cup butter
2 teaspoons salt
1 teaspoon baking powder
2 1/2 cups masa harina mix
3/4 cup sugar
1 teaspoon cinnamon
1 1/2 cups water
2/3 cup raisins
2/3 cup finely chopped almonds
1/4 cup sweet cream

red food coloring (optional)

Soak husks according to the instructions given for *Tamales* (p.35)

Beat the butter until light and fluffy. In a large bowl, mix the masa harina, salt, baking powder, sugar and cinnamon. Add the water a little bit at a time, beating after each addition. Add the beaten butter, a little at a time, beating after each addition. Beat in a few drops of red food coloring if the traditional pink color for sweet tamales is desired.

Mix the raisins, almonds and sweet cream to make the filling. Proceed as directed in the basic *Tamales* recipe for assembling and steaming the tamales. Makes 24.

Champurrado
Hot Chocolate Drink

Champurrado and its cousin, *atole*, fall into a category of nourishing drinks based on thin corn gruel, yet another culinary use of corn in Mexico. This particular beverage brings together corn and chocolate, another Mesoamerican native.

The ninth century pre-Hispanic archeological site Cacaxtla, in central Puebla, was a trade depot for Mayan cacao merchants from the lowlands, who are portrayed with their loads of beans in bright frescos on the walls of the buildings. Each load of cacao beans, which had to be imported to this cool, dry area from the coastal lowlands, contained 24,000 beans, carefully counted one by one because they were so valuable that they were used as coins.

Although certainly no longer recognized as currency, cocoa beans and their numerous derivative chocolate products are still used in Mexico primarily as beverages such as the beloved *champurrado*. As an early morning drink, it is filling enough to tide one over until a more solid meal is forthcoming. At night, it is perfect for those who wish to avoid eating a late supper, without going to bed on an empty stomach.

Ingredients:

1/3 cup masa harina mix
4 cups cold water
2 tablets Mexican chocolate (4 ounces)
1 stick cinnamon
2 tablespoons dark brown sugar or piloncillo, or to taste
Milk, to taste

In a medium saucepan, dissolve the masa harina mix in the water and cook, stirring, over medium heat until the mixture reaches the consistency of heavy cream. Strain it into a larger saucepan, add the remaining ingredients and cook, stirring constantly over medium heat until the chocolate and sugar have dissolved. The *champurrado* may be thinned with milk if desired. Serve hot in mugs. Serves 4.

Pambazos
Hot Savory Sandwiches

On Sunday nights, families congregate in and around the main plaza, called the *zócalo*, in nearly every town in Mexico. Each one has its late night snack specialties. In Cholula, a favorite is *pambazo*, a soft sandwich-sized roll filled with shredded chicken, topped with a savory sauce and garnished with slices of avocado and onion. On the feast day of the patroness of our neighborhood, Nuestra Señora de Dolores, there is a small carnival featuring rides and food booths which fill the narrow streets surrounding the local church. Although the carnival falls on a meatless Lenten Friday, everyone still gets to enjoy *pambazos*, which are equally good stuffed with the Oaxacan string cheese called *quesillo*. Drenched with the warm sauce, they make a good light supper on a chilly night. *Pambazo* rolls are softer than regular Mexican *bolillos*, so use bread rolls rather than French rolls. This sauce may be frozen in small containers for quick meals as needed.

Ingredients:

For the *Pambazos*:

8 soft rolls, split and hollowed out slightly
2 chicken breasts, cooked and shredded, or shredded
Oaxaca cheese
2 avocadoes, peeled and sliced
1 large white onion, sliced into thin rings
1 recipe *pambazo* sauce, below

For the sauce:

1 lb. roma tomatoes
2 1/2 ounces guajillo chiles, seeded and deveined
1/8 teaspoon cumin
2 whole cloves
2 whole allspice berries
1/2 teaspoon oregano
1/2 cinnamon stick
1/2 medium white onion, peeled and grated
1 clove garlic, crushed
1 1/2 tablespoons lard or corn oil
salt to taste

Make the sauce by placing the tomatoes, chiles and spices in a medium saucepan with water just to cover. Boil until the tomatoes are soft, liquefy in a blender, strain through a sieve, and set aside. Heat the oil or lard, add the onion and garlic and cook over medium heat until the onion is soft. Add the strained tomato mixture and cook until slightly thickened, 15-20 minutes.

Assemble the sandwiches by filling the rolls with the chicken or cheese, ladling warm sauce over all, and topping with the avocado and onion. Makes 8 *pambazos*.

Quesadillas de Huitlacoche
Huitlacoche Quesadillas

The heavy rainy season in Central Mexico creates ideal conditions for the growth of a fungus on the corn. The botanical name for this corn "smut" is *ustilago maydis*, but it is far more commonly known by its Nahuatl name, *huitlacoche*. Essentially a mushroom, it is particularly prized in the central Mexican highlands, with a sufficient demand to support an industry that grows and cans it. Proof of its increasing popularity north of the border is the fact that some US farmers are attempting to grow corn with large infestations of *ustilago maydis* because US demand makes the fungus a more valuable cash crop than the corn on which it grows.

The taste of *huitlacoche* has been compared to that of morels. The earthy mushroom flavor and the hint of corn taste are a unique combination, delicious in quesadillas, because the mildness of the cheese is a perfect foil for the rich taste of *huitlacoche*. The quesadilla stands in the markets always feature it as one of the fillings during the rainy season. While you probably won't find it sold fresh outside Mexico, it is often found canned, under the brand name Hérdez, in Latin markets. The *huitlacoche* sauce in the following recipe can also be used to top eggs, to fill crepes or served with grilled meat or chicken.

Ingredients:

> 2 lbs. *huitlacoche*, or two cans (210 grams, or
> approximately 7 ounces, each)
> 2-3 tablespoons corn oil
> 2 small poblano chiles, roasted, peeled, seeded and diced
> 1/2 medium white onion, chopped
> 2 cloves garlic, chopped
> 1 sprig of epazote, chopped
> salt to taste
> 8 large corn tortillas
> 2 cups shredded mild cheese, such as manchego or
> Monterrey Jack

If using fresh *huitlacoche*, chop it coarsely and set it aside.

Heat the oil in a large skillet and sauté the chile, onion and garlic over medium heat until the onion is soft. Add the huitlacoche, epazote and salt and continue cooking until the huitlacoche is soft and renders its juices. Cooking time will be shorter for canned huitlacoche.

Heat the tortillas on both sides on a dry griddle or *comal.* Evenly distribute the cheese on one half of each tortilla, top the cheese with the huitlacoche sauce, and fold the tortillas to form quesadillas. Cook on both sides until the cheese melts. Makes 8.

Enchiladas Dobladas
Folded Enchiladas

In Mexico, enchiladas take on many forms, from the *enchiladas mineras* ("miners' enchiladas") of Guanajuato, to *enchiladas suizas*, "Swiss enchiladas", featuring *salsa verde* and garnished with cream. Although many US recipes call for baking enchiladas, this is not a traditional preparation. Rather, the tortillas are soft fried in lard or oil, dipped in sauce, filled and garnished with cheese and onions.

One of my fondest memories is getting on the train for a ride through the central Puebla countryside right after the rainy season, back when the trains still ran. The tracks went through fields of flowers and passed turn-of-the-century train stations, their columns covered with morning glory vines. At every stop, people hawking food and drink boarded the train. We always looked for the "enchilada ladies", who carried their wares in large, flat baskets and passed them out on butcher paper. They were messy to eat that way, but definitely worth every drip.

Ingredients:

For the enchiladas:

12 large corn tortillas
4 tablespoons lard or oil
2 cups *queso fresco*, farmer's cheese or mild feta, crumbled
1/2 medium white onion, chopped
1/2 cup crème fraîche or Mexican *crema*
1 recipe enchilada sauce, below

For the enchilada sauce:

6 roma tomatoes

3 ancho chiles, seeded, deveined, lightly toasted and soaked until softened

3 pasilla chiles, seeded, deveined, lightly toasted and soaked until softened

2 canned chipotles in adobo sauce

1/2 medium white onion, peeled and chopped

2 large cloves garlic, peeled

2 tablespoons lard or corn oil

salt to taste

Make the sauce by roasting the tomatoes on a griddle or *comal* until the skins blister and placing them in the blender with the chiles, onions, garlic and one cup of the water in which the chiles were soaked; puree. Heat the lard or corn oil in a medium saucepan and add the chile-tomato puree. Cook over medium heat for 20 minutes and season to taste.

To assemble the enchiladas, heat the oil or lard in a frying pan until a few drops of water sprinkled in it jump around. If the oil is not hot enough, the tortillas will absorb too much of it. Soft-fry the tortillas for a few seconds on each side and drain on paper towels. Dip the tortillas in the simmering enchilada sauce, sprinkle half the cheese and onion lightly over them, fold them in half and then in half again. Ladle remaining chile sauce over them, and sprinkle with remaining cheese and onion. Drizzle the cream mixture over them and serve immediately. Makes 12.

Chileatole
Corn and Chile Soup

Chileatole, a thick soup flavored with green chiles, mainly uses ingredients that were found in Mexico before the Spaniards arrived. In this sense, it is quite typical of food in this part of the state. It takes its name from the chiles with which it is flavored and *atole*, derived from the Nauhuatl word *atolli*, a thick corn soup or drink. *Chileatole*, besides being delicious, has been used as a cure for colds since the time of the Aztec Empire. It is a warming comfort food in a cool, mountain climate, usually sold at night in the streets around the markets.

Ingredients:

1/3 cup corn oil
1 medium white onion, peeled and grated
4 large garlic cloves, crushed
8 fresh ears of corn, kernels removed
8 1/2 cups homemade chicken or vegetable broth
1 1/4 cups *masa harina* mixed with 3/4-1 cup water to form a smooth dough
6 poblano chiles, roasted, seeded and peeled
3 serrano chiles, lightly roasted
4 sprigs epazote
4 *hoja santa* leaves or 8 sprigs cilantro, chopped
salt to taste

In a stockpot, heat the corn oil and add the onion, garlic and corn kernels. Cook over medium heat for 10 minutes, stirring occasionally. Add 4 cups of the broth, cover and simmer until the vegetables are tender.

Dissolve the corn dough in 4 cups of the broth, strain through a sieve and add to the vegetables. Cover and cook over low heat for 45 minutes, stirring occasionally.

Put the chiles in a blender with the remaining 1/2 cup of broth and puree. Add the chiles, chopped *hoja santa* or cilantro, and salt to taste. The soup should be fairly thick. Continue cooking for 5 more minutes and serve hot, garnished with fried tortilla strips if desired. Serves 8-10.

Crema de Flor de Calabaza
Squash Blossom Soup

Calabacitas, or zucchini, are one of the most common vegetables in the region, and their blossoms are used in soups, sauces and for stuffing and batter-dipping. This recipe was given to me by Isabel Hoyos Gomez, a good friend and the first person in Mexico to let me loose in her kitchen. It can be made ahead of time, but do not add the cream until just before heating.

Ingredients:

> 2 tablespoons butter
> 1 medium white onion, peeled and chopped
> 2 large cloves garlic, peeled and chopped
> 2 roma tomatoes, roasted, peeled, seeded and chopped
> 1 1/2 lbs. squash blossoms, cleaned
> 6 cups homemade chicken broth (p.20)
> 3/4 cups Mexican *crema* or heavy cream
> salt to taste

Melt the butter in a medium sauce pan, add the onion and garlic and sauté until soft. Add the tomatoes and squash blossoms and cook over medium heat for 15 minutes. Puree the vegetables in a blender with a little of the chicken broth until smooth. Return to the saucepan, add the rest of the broth and salt to taste. Bring to a boil, lower the heat and simmer, uncovered, another 10 minutes. Slowly stir in the cream and continue cooking until slightly thickened, but do not allow the soup to boil once the cream has been added. Serve hot, garnished with strips of roasted poblano chile if desired. Serves 6

Champiñones al Ajillo
Mushrooms with Garlic and Chile

Guajillo chiles play a dual role as flavoring and garnish in this recipe, which comes from Chialingo's, a restaurant in Cholula featuring regional cuisine. It can be served as an appetizer or side dish, with a basket of small, warm corn tortillas. The guajillo chile rings will remain slightly chewy, providing a nice textural contrast with the *champiñones*. Button mushrooms are best in this dish, since their taste is mild enough not to compete with the garlic and chile. In any case, canned mushrooms cannot be substituted for fresh.

Ingredients:

> 1/2 lb. fresh button mushrooms
> 3 tablespoons olive oil
> 3-4 large cloves garlic, chopped
> 3-4 guajillo chiles, stemmed, seeded and cut into thin rings
> salt to taste

Cut the mushrooms into fourths, including the stems. In a medium skillet, heat the olive oil to the point of fragrance and add the garlic. Sauté just until the garlic begins to soften, add the mushrooms and chile rings, saving a few chile rings for garnish. Continue to sauté, over medium heat, until the mushrooms release their juice. Salt to taste and serve immediately. Serves 4 as an appetizer with tortillas.

Arroz Blanco Con Verduras
White Rice with Vegetables

The vegetables used in this recipe are all in season at the same time, which may be why they complement each other so well. Fresh white corn, rather than yellow, makes a big difference in the taste. Mexican corn has an earthier flavor and is more suitable for mixing with other vegetables than the hybrid sweet corn, which tastes to me like it has sugar added. No matter which you choose to use, it is important that the vegetables be fresh, since rice absorbs the flavors that surround it.

Ingredients:

> 2 tablespoons corn oil
> 1/2 medium white onion, peeled and chopped
> 2 large cloves garlic, peeled and chopped
> 1/4 lb. fresh mushrooms, coarsely chopped
> 1 cup long grain rice, soaked in warm water, rinsed and allowed to dry thoroughly
> 1 cup white corn, freshly cut from the cob
> 2 small poblano chiles, roasted, seeded, peeled, and cut into 1/2" squares
> 2 1/2 tablespoons chopped fresh epazote
> 2 1/2 cups hot homemade chicken broth

Heat the oil in a heavy saucepan or *cazuela*, add the onion and garlic and sauté 3-4 minutes. Add the mushrooms and sauté another 3-4 minutes. Add the rice and cook, stirring from time to time to prevent sticking. The rice will form small clumps at first and then separate into individual grains. When the rice has turned pale gold in color, stir in the corn, chiles and epazote. Add the hot broth, bring to a boil, lower heat and simmer, covered, until the liquid has been absorbed. Serves 6 as a side dish or *sopa seca* course.

Ensalada de Nopalitos
Nopales Salad

Mexican markets are as intriguing today as they were when the Spaniards discovered them, with their huge assortment of fruits and vegetables arranged in neat stacks. The prickly pear, a member of the *opuntia* genus which produces the vegetables called *nopales* and the fruit called *tuna*, is sold cleaned of its spines and often sliced into small squares.

This versatile plant, used in soups, stews, casseroles and salads, dots the landscape all over Central Mexico, and is found in abundance at virtually every pre-Hispanic archeological site in the area. An important staple in the diet of the Mesoamericans, nopales have to be eaten, or cooked, soon after they are picked.

That is why women in the markets are usually busy scraping the glochids, or thorns, called *agüates* in Mexico, off the freshly picked vegetables to ready them for the day's shoppers. Nutritious and versatile, they are sold for literally just pennies. Their taste when cooked is quite similar to green beans and their texture, if not cooked long enough, similar to okra. They are a natural weight-control food and are sold in dehydrated form in health food stores.

The central Puebla town of Tlaxcalancingo produces so many that they have a *nopal* festival each year. This *pueblito* is just a few miles from the Puebla city limits, but looks like a painting from an antique Mexican calendar. Set against a backdrop of snow-covered volcanoes, amidst fields of prickly pears, the town celebrates its spiny harvest with specialties of every imaginable kind, including *nopal* ice cream.

The following salad can be used as a garnish on tacos and tostadas, and is a good accompaniment to grilled meat, chicken or fish.

Ingredients:

> 3 cups diced nopal cactus paddles
> 1/2 cup finely chopped white onion
> 1/2 cup finely chopped small red radishes
> 1/4 cup finely chopped cilantro leaves
> 3 tablespoons olive oil
> juice of 1 fresh lime
> 1/4 teaspoon crumbled dried oregano leaves (Mexican oregano if possible)
> salt and pepper to taste

Place the diced nopales in a large pot with water to cover, bring to a boil and continue boiling for 30 minutes. To ensure that the sticky juice is extracted completely, some Mexican cooks add a few tomatillo husks and others a pinch of baking soda. Care must be used if adding baking soda, since it will cause the water to foam up and possibly overflow the pot. Drain the nopales in a colander and rinse them under cold water. Place them in a bowl with the remaining ingredients and toss to blend well. Let the salad stand for one hour before serving. Serves 4-6.

Huaraches
Stuffed Nopales

We first tried these at the *Festival de Nopales* in Tlaxcalancingo. The señora who was making them had a pile of the biggest nopal paddles I have ever seen, pre-boiled and ready to be made into *huaraches*, aptly named for the flat soles of the country people's sandals that they resemble.

Nopales are also delicious grilled. Cut them from the wide, rounded end toward, but not all to way to, the narrow end, fanning out the cuts so that the paddles look fringed. Brush them with olive oil or a flavored oil of your choice and grill until soft and slightly charred. This is one of the requisite elements of a *parrillada*, a Mexican "mixed grill."

Ingredients:

> 6 large nopal cactus paddles
> 1/4 medium white onion
> 1 large garlic clove, peeled and cut in half
> salt to taste
> 6 slices manchego, Monterrey Jack or Gouda cheese
> 1/4 - 1/2 cup flour
> 3 eggs, separated and at room temperature
> 1/2 cup corn oil

Place the whole cactus paddles, onion and garlic in a large pot with water to cover and salt to taste. Boil for approximately 30 minutes, or until the nopales are tender but still firm. Drain and rinse. Starting at the wide, curved end, carefully slice each paddle horizontally, as though butterflying a chop for stuffing. Do not cut all the way through to the narrow end (the thicker part where the paddle is attached to the plant) but leave approximately 1 1/2" uncut. Place a slice of cheese between the two sections, and press flat.

Dredge the paddles in flour. Beat the egg whites until they form stiff peaks, and fold in the lightly beaten yolks. Heat oil in a large skillet until a few drops of water sprinkled into it bounce. Dredge the stuffed nopal paddles in the egg batter and fry until golden brown on each side. Serve immediately with tomato sauce or red salsa. Serves 6.

Rajas con Crema
Poblano Chile Strips with Cream

In late summer, when the dark green, glossy poblano chiles are piled high in the market, and the prices drop proportionally, I usually end up buying kilos of them, for stuffing, for use in soups, stews and salsas, and for making *rajas con crema*. This versatile recipe can be used as a vegetable side dish, as a filling for tamales, or used to fill crepes.

    1/3 cup butter
    1/3 cup corn oil
    2 large white onions, peeled and sliced into half moons
    2 large cloves garlic, peeled and minced
    12 poblano chiles, roasted, peeled, seeded, and sliced into
    strips
    2 cups Mexican *crema* or heavy cream
    Salt to taste

Melt the butter in a large skillet, add the onion and garlic and cook until the onion is transparent. Add the chiles, cream and salt to taste; cook over low heat until the mixture is heated through. Serves 6-8 as a side dish.

Pipian Verde
Chicken in Green Pumpkin Seed Sauce

While a *mole* does not necessarily have seeds, a *pipian* does; the green ones always contain ground pumpkin seeds. *Pipian verde* is probably the main dish most associated with the central region of Puebla. It is so frequently prepared that it can be found in the form of a "convenience food" of sorts, with the pumpkin seeds sold in the market spice stalls already ground into a paste with the seasonings. It is not difficult to make, however, and once made the sauce can be frozen. It can also be used, combined with some of the cooked chicken or meat, in tamales. If you have never tried making a *mole* or *pipian*, this is a good one to start with; a comparatively minimal amount of preparation produces rewarding results. Pork and its broth may be used instead of chicken.

Ingredients:

For the chicken:
1 whole chicken, cut into serving pieces
1/2 medium white onion, peeled
2 cloves garlic, peeled and cut in half
1 medium carrot, cut into chunks
1 bay leaf
6 whole black peppercorns
2 whole cloves
2 allspice berries
salt to taste

For the sauce:

3/4 cup hulled pumpkin seeds
8 medium-size tomatillos
1/2 medium onion, peeled and coarsely chopped
2 large cloves garlic, peeled and halved
2-4 serrano chiles, depending on the degree of heat desired
4 poblano chiles, roasted, peeled, seeded and chopped
4 romaine lettuce leaves
3 sprigs cilantro
3 sprigs epazote (parsley may be used instead)
4 cups stock, strained, from cooking the chicken or meat
2 tablespoons lard or corn oil
salt to taste

Place the chicken, onion, garlic, carrot, bay leaf, peppercorns, cloves, allspice berries and salt to taste in a stockpot with water to cover. Cook, covered, until tender, about 40 minutes, removing white meat of chicken after 25-30 minutes so that it does not become rubbery. Remove from heat, strain stock and set the chicken aside.

In a hot, dry frying pan, toast the pumpkin seeds just until they pop, taking care not to burn them. This is best accomplished by shaking the pan as they pop. Remove them from the heat and allow them to cool. Grind them as finely as possible in a spice grinder or *molcajete*.

Put the tomatillos, onion, garlic and serranos in a medium saucepan with 2 cups of the strained broth. Bring to a boil and simmer until the tomatillos become soft. Transfer this to a blender, add the chopped poblanos and lettuce and puree until smooth. Add the ground pumpkin seeds, cilantro and epazote or parsley and puree again. Heat the lard or corn oil in a large, heavy saucepan or *cazuela* and add the blended ingredients. Add the remaining 2 cups stock gradually, stirring continuously.

Simmer over low heat for 30 minutes, stirring frequently to make sure that the sauce does not burn or stick. Taste for salt. Serve in soup bowls, placing a piece of chicken in each bowl and ladling the sauce over it. Accompany with rice and warm corn tortillas. Serves 6.

Variation: **Pipian Verde Vegetariano**: Follow the recipe above, using vegetable broth and an equivalent amount of vegetables to replace the chicken. Good choices are cobs of corn cut into fourths, along with potatoes, carrots, and chayote, all cut chunk-style. Zucchini, which becomes mushy if overcooked, may be added when the other vegetables are nearly done.

Pollo Poblano:
Chicken in Poblano Cream Sauce

This dish is popular for big parties because it can be made in large quantities while keeping the same proportions. The sauce can be made ahead, and the recipe assembled quickly. It is one of the few instances where poblano chiles are used without having to be roasted and peeled. The poblano cream sauce is excellent for topping crepes filled with mushrooms or huitlacoche, or for mixing with cooked pasta, topped with cheese and popped in the oven until the cheese melts.

Ingredients:

> 3-4 poblano chiles, seeded and chopped
> 1/2 cup milk
> 4 tablespoons butter
> 2 tablespoons flour
> 1 cup thick cream (Mexican *crema* or heavy cream)
> salt to taste
> 2 whole chicken breasts, cut in half
> 1 cup grated manchego, Monterrey Jack or Gouda cheese

Puree the chiles in a blender with the milk until smooth. In a medium saucepan, melt 2 tablespoons of the butter, add the flour and brown lightly. Add the chile puree, stirring with a wooden spoon or wire whisk until smooth. Add the cream, stirring constantly over low heat until it just begins to bubble. Remove from the heat and add salt to taste. This sauce may be made one day in advance and refrigerated.

Melt the remaining 2 tablespoons of butter in a medium skillet, and sauté chicken breast halves for 4 minutes on each side. Place them in a buttered baking dish, pour the poblano cream sauce over all, top with the grated cheese and bake uncovered in a preheated oven at 350° for 20 minutes, at which time the cheese will be golden and bubbly. Serves 4.

Pollo Atlixquense
Grilled Marinated Chicken Breasts

The town of Atlizco, said to have one of the best climates in the world, is situated in a beautiful valley in the center of the state. Famous for its extensive cultivation of flowers, Atlizco was the subject of dispute among pre-Hispanic indigenous groups, all of whom wanted to annex it. The matter was settled when it was claimed for the Spanish crown in 1579.

The town is famous for the chicken dish named after it, flavored with *criollo* avocado leaves. The *criollo* variety is prized for its thin, dark, anise-flavored skin and its fragrant leaves. The leaves are dried and used as a seasoning in many foods typical of the central Puebla area. In this dish, they are ground and used to flavor a unique and delicious marinade.

Ingredients:

> 4 boneless, skinless chicken breasts, cut in half
> 4 large cloves garlic, peeled and crushed
> 1/2 medium white onion, grated
> 8 dried *criollo* avocado leaves, lightly toasted and ground
> 8 tablespoons melted butter
> 1/4 cup olive oil
> 1/2 teaspoon freshly ground black pepper
> salt to taste
> 6 cups home made chicken broth, simmered until reduced
> to 2 cups

Place the chicken in a glass baking dish. In a small bowl, mix the onion, garlic, half the ground avocado leaves, half the butter, half the olive oil, the black pepper and salt to taste . Pour marinade over chicken, cover and let rest for at least 2 hours, turning once.

In a medium saucepan, heat the remaining half of the butter and olive oil, add the remaining half of the ground avocado leaves and stir. Pour in the reduced chicken broth and stir with a wire whisk until the sauce is emulsified. Set aside.

Grill the chicken over hot coals or on a stove top grill, brushing with the marinade,   until cooked through. Discard any remaining marinade. Heat the sauce and serve the grilled chicken bathed in the sauce. Serves 8.

Carne de Cerdo en Adobo
Pork in Adobo Sauce

The Spanish influence on Puebla's homes is visible to the extent that the houses are hidden from the street. You never know what lies behind the high walls and metal gates, unless the aroma indicates that the residents keep pigs. Along with chicken, pork is the most frequently consumed meat in the central Puebla region. Food is never thrown away, and fruit and vegetable peelings, along with stale tortillas, comprise the main portion of the pigs' diet. It must be a healthy one, because the meat is lean and tasty. This *adobo*, with its use of chocolate, is typical of the Puebla area.

Ingredients:

> 1 lb. boneless pork, cut into small cubes
> water to cover
> salt and pepper to taste
> 2 ancho chiles, seeded, deveined, and lightly toasted
> 1 pasilla chile, seeded, deveined, and lightly toasted
> 1/2 white onion, peeled
> 2 large cloves garlic, peeled
> 4 black peppercorns
> 2 whole cloves
> 1/2 cinnamon stick or 1/4 teaspoon ground cinnamon
> 2 tablespoons vinegar
> 1 ounce Mexican chocolate (1/2 tablet)
> 2 tablespoons lard or corn oil
> salt and pepper to taste

Place the meat, water to cover, salt and pepper to taste in a large heavy-bottomed pot or *cazuela*. Cover and cook until tender. The broth should be nearly all absorbed. Remove the meat and set aside.

Soak the chiles in warm water to cover until soft. Grind them with the onion, garlic, peppercorns, cloves, cinnamon, vinegar and chocolate in a *molcajete* or in a blender with just enough of the soaking liquid to allow movement of the blades.

In the same pot in which the meat was cooked, heat the lard or oil, add the meat and brown slowly until golden. Add the adobo sauce and continue cooking for 10 more minutes, or until the meat is dark red and glazed. Serve on a platter with sliced onion, lettuce and radishes, accompanied by warm corn tortillas. Serves 4.

Rosca de Reyes
Three Kings Cake

Señor Jose Dominguez, known to friends and clients of the *Panadería Chiquita* ("The Little Bakery") as Don Pepe, has been baking bread since he was eight years old, apprenticing in his father's bakery in Cholula. His father had learned from his father before him, and started young Pepe literally from the ground up; his job was to gather wood for the oven fire, get it going and maintain it at an even temperature.

Don Pepe still uses the traditional brick oven and wood fire for baking. He is an advocate of preserving as many traditions as possible, and was one of the founders of the Cholula Bread Fair, held each October, during which a huge brick oven is constructed in the plaza and bread-making demonstrations are given.

In *La Chiquita*, I learned to make, among other things, cake for Three Kings Day, celebrated on January 6th to honor the gift-bearing Magi. On this day, children receive toys, and this cake is served at parties. A miniature doll, representing the Christ child, is baked into the bread, and tradition holds that whoever gets the slice of *rosca* with the doll in it has to provide the tamales and *atole* for the next party, on Candlemas. This is a yeast cake, of the type that would be called a coffee cake in the US, and can be kneaded by hand or with a mixer with a kneading attachment.

Ingredients:

For the starter dough:

1/4 cup flour
3 tablespoons active dry yeast

3 tablespoons sugar
1/8 teaspoon salt
warm water

For the dough:

2 cups flour
3/4 cup butter, softened
8 egg yolks
4 whole eggs
1/2 cup sugar
1/8 teaspoon salt
zest of 2 oranges
1/2 cup chopped walnuts
1/4 cup raisins
1/4 cup dried figs
1 miniature plastic or porcelain doll

For the decoration:

2 beaten eggs
2 figs, cut in strips
1 candied citron, cut in strips
sugar to taste

For the starter dough, mix the flour, yeast, sugar, salt and enough warm water to form a soft, moist ball. Cover and let it stand in a draft-free place for one hour.

For the dough, place the flour on a clean, dry surface, leaving a well in the middle. Mix the butter, egg yolks, eggs, sugar, salt and orange zest and pour the mixture into the well. Slowly incorporate the flour into the mixture until a dough of uniform consistency has been formed. Add the starter dough and knead until the dough is smooth and not sticky. Place the dough in a greased bowl, cover with a clean cloth and leave it to rise in a warm, draft-free place for 2 hours, or until doubled in volume.

On a clean, dry surface, extend the dough into a rectangle and place a row of walnuts, raisins and figs on the dough, along with the doll. Fold the dough over once, and form into a ring by joining the ends. Place the *rosca* on a greased baking sheet and brush it with the beaten eggs. Place the fig and candied citron strips on top, and sprinkle with sugar. Let it sit at room temperature for 15 minutes, then bake in a preheated 350° oven for 25 minutes, or until golden brown. Serves 10.

Figuritas de Almendra
Almond Paste Candies

Almond paste candies are very popular in Mexico, especially in the Puebla region, where they are sold at fairs and on holidays by vendors who walk around with huge trays of them, most often shaped like chickens. Why chickens? I've asked and received the reply that it is just traditional. I would like to pursue that further, but meanwhile I shape them as hearts and give them as Valentine's Day gifts.

Ingredients:

> 10 ounces blanched almonds
> 10 ounces confectioners' sugar
> 1 egg white
> 1 teaspoon almond extract
> red food coloring (optional)

Grind the almonds to a paste and mix thoroughly with the powdered sugar. Place the mixture in a blender or food processor with the egg white and the almond extract; blend or process until a paste is formed. If it seems to thin to handle, add a bit more confectioners' sugar; if too thick, add a few drops of lime juice.

Knead the paste for a few minutes and mold it into desired shapes - hearts, fruit, etc. The *figuritas* can be colored with a little food coloring diluted in water, or rolled in powdered sugar. If they are to be given as gifts, wrap them individually in tissue paper.

Ponche Navideño
Holiday Punch

In the busy central Puebla market town of San Martin Texmelucan, hot fruit punch is sold at night by street vendors who ladle it out from steaming cylindrical vats. *Ponche* was probably invented as a hot drink because the fruits which are its main ingredients are in season during the chilly winter months. It is almost always associated with the Christmas and New Year holiday season, when it is served "spiked" at parties. The *tejocote* is a small fruit, golden in color when mature, resembling an apple, with a similar taste but a pastier texture. The *tejocote* is not easily found outside Mexico; however, apples make a good substitute without changing the essential character of *ponche.*

Ingredients:

> 6 large Golden Delicious apples, cored and sliced (or 3/4 lb. *tejocote*, if available)
> 10 guavas, halved
> 1/2 lb. raisins, prunes, or a mixture of both
> 6 oranges, scrubbed and sliced with rind
> 4 pieces sugar cane stalk, peeled and cut into strips
> 2 sticks cinnamon
> water to cover
> sugar to taste (about 1/3 cup to each quart of water)
> 1 bottle brandy, rum or red wine, or to taste (optional)

Place the apples, guavas, raisins, prunes, oranges, sugar cane and cinnamon in a large stockpot with water to cover. Bring to a boil, lower heat, cover and simmer one hour. Add sugar to taste, along with brandy, rum or wine if desired; cover and simmer another10 minutes. Serve hot in mugs.

canastas con frutas

CHAPTER IV

La Sierra Mágica:
Beauty and Bounty

The Sierra Madre Oriental, the eastern mountain range which separates Puebla from its coastal neighbor, Veracruz, is home to a large indigenous population, predominantly Totonac and Nahua. Guardians of pre-Hispanic recipes and cooking secrets, the inhabitants of the *sierra* use the abundance of fruit produced in their vast orchards to make preserves and wines. Apples, plums, cherries and blackberries are just a few of the many varieties with which the famous *vinos de fruta* are made.

The mountain streams of this beautiful region contain trout and other fish which are grilled, baked, poached, and used to fill tamales and chiles. Before the arrival of the Spaniards, with their lard and olive oil, food was not fried but grilled over coals, boiled, or baked on a *comal*.

The aromas of anise and coffee fill the clean mountain air, and coffee beans can be seen spread out on patios to dry. The eastern slope of the *sierra* has the perfect combination of high altitude and moist air from the Gulf of Mexico for optimal coffee growing conditions.

The farmers who tend coffee and other crops still wear the same pleated white cotton shirt and loose-fitting pants as they have for hundreds of years, and their wives the white dresses with flower-embroidered yokes that appear spotless in even the muddiest weather. This is one of the few remaining regions of Puebla where the inhabitants wear their traditional dress on a daily basis rather than just for *fiestas*. The upswept hairdo worn by the women, with intricate coils wrapped in purple yarn, is the same one used by their pre-Hispanic ancestors.

Those same forebears learned how to cultivate and use aromatic plants native to the area. Allspice and vanilla abound here, with vanilla seed pods spread out to dry in the same manner as the coffee beans. The vanilla plant itself, a tropical orchid native to Mexico, does not have a noticeable scent. The seed pod, or vanilla bean, acquires its distinctive perfume only after drying in the sun or over wood fires, followed by months of special conditioning. The cultivation of the orchid, as well as the curing of the bean, was kept undisclosed to the conquistadores, and the natives were said to have screamed out frightening oaths to prevent their knowledge from being spread.

The people of the *sierra* travel to other parts of the state with delicacies from the area; a booth with fruit preserves and wines can be seen at nearly every local fair in the state of Puebla. The Totonacs from the high tropical region of the mountains bordering Veracruz walk through the crowds selling bottles of pure vanilla extract or small figures - butterflies, birds, flowers - formed by artfully twisting the long beans together to be used as sachets.

These vendors are always happy to meet people who have visited their towns, villages and countryside. We are not just being polite when we tell them that we have fond memories of the morning mists, the bright, clear days, the ancient pyramids and hauntingly beautiful old churches. We have never left the *Sierra Magica* without planning to return.

Tlacoyos
Bean-Stuffed Corn Cakes

These are somewhat akin to the thick, stuffed corncakes called *gorditas*. The traditional filling in the *sierra* is *arvejón*, a small legume, but other types of beans work well. *Tlacoyos* are generally made with blue corn flour, increasingly available as blue masa harina mix outside Mexico. Yellow or white masa work as well. *Tlacoyos* are baked, rather than fried, on a hot griddle or *comal*, making them naturally low in fat. They are served spread with *salsa de jitomate* (below) and topped with a sprinkling of cheese.

Ingredients:

> 1 1/2 lbs. *masa* (see Index)
> 1/2 lb. dried beans
> 2 dried avocado leaves
> salt to taste
> 3 ounces lard or vegetable shortening
> 1 recipe *Salsa de Jitomate* (below)
> Crumbled farmers' cheese, mild feta or *queso fresco* for garnish

Shape the masa into 10 large, thick tortillas. Boil the beans with the avocado leaves and salt to taste until tender, strain and mash to a paste. Beat in the lard or vegetable oil and spread some of the bean mixture on the center of each tortilla. Fold the tortilla over and pinch the edges together, stretching it out to form an oval shape. Heat a dry griddle or comal and bake on each side until cooked through. This should take only a few minutes on each side if the griddle is hot enough. Spread *salsa de jitomate* on each *tlacoyo* and sprinkle with crumbled cheese. Makes 10.

Salsa de Jitomate
Roasted Tomato Salsa

The town of Cuetzalan, in the coffee growing region of the *sierra*, draws many visitors year round, thanks to its freshly roasted gourmet coffee beans, beautifully hand-embroidered clothes and table linens, and delicious variety of tasty snacks prepared by the women who set up their charcoal braziers and comals in the central plaza in the evening. Set at the bottom of steps which connect it to the town's narrow, cobbled streets, the plaza is the place where people converge after the sun goes down to gossip, flirt, or watch their children at play. This salsa is the condiment of choice for the myriad night time nibbles, and has been since pre-Hispanic times, when the very same ingredients were ground in *molcajetes*. Whether you choose to use a molcajete, a blender or a food processor, it is important to grind the ingredients in the order listed and to avoid over-processing. All ingredients should be roasted on a hot comal or griddle.

Ingredients:

> 3 large garlic cloves, roasted in their skins, then peeled
> salt to taste
> 1/2 large white onion, peeled and chopped
> 4 serrano chiles, or more to taste, lightly roasted
> 1 lb. roma tomatoes, roasted, unpeeled
> water as necessary

Grind the garlic and salt together, adding the onion and chile next, then gradually add the tomatoes, using only enough water necessary to thin the salsa to the desired consistency. If ground in a molcajete, this salsa can be brought directly to the table in it.

Molotes Poblanos
Fried Stuffed Quesadillas

Molotes are a snack food found in several regions of Mexico, but the biggest ones are made in the state of Puebla. In *The Hungry Traveler: Mexico*, Marita Adair writes that "Puebla offers the King Kong of molotes." In the *sierra* region, *molote* ladies can be found day and night, forming the ovals of thin corn dough, sealing the edges over the filling and frying them in hot oil to a golden crispness, while the hungry customer watches every step eagerly. Cheese, squash blossoms, mushrooms, chorizo and tinga are the traditional *poblano* fillings for molotes.

Ingredients:

> 1 lb corn masa (Chapter V)
> warm water
> salt to taste
> 1/4 cup lard or vegetable oil
> Filling: tinga (Chapter II), wild mushrooms with epazote
> (Chapter II), fried chorizo sausage, fresh squash blossoms,
> or shredded cheese

Knead the masa with enough water, plus salt to taste, to form a smooth, firm dough. The dough should be kneaded until no longer sticky. Leave it to rest in a bowl, covered with a damp cloth, for 15 minutes. Line a tortilla press with squares of waxed paper and pinch off egg-size balls of dough. Place each ball in the tortilla press and flatten to make a large, thin tortilla about 7"-8" in diameter.

Carefully peel off the waxed paper and gently stretch the tortilla into an oblong shape. Place some filling down the center, fold in half and pinch the edges shut.

Heat the oil in a large skillet and fry each molote, turning once, until crisp and golden brown on both sides. Makes 12.

Huevos Zacatlantecos
Eggs with Sautéed Apples and Parsley

Famous for its orchards, Zacatlán celebrates the fruit harvest in August, with a big festival starting on the 15th, to celebrate the feast day of the Virgin of the Ascension, who has taken the place of the ancient harvest goddess as patroness of the town. The statue of the Virgin is dressed in embroidered white satin and lace and laid on a bed of green apples piled before the altar of the parish church. Every hour throughout the night the statue is raised a little higher until, by 12 a.m., it is upright. The Virgin is then taken on a procession through the streets, accompanied by music and fireworks. Thus begins a week of celebration including dances, rodeos, parades with floats and lots of good food. Piles of fresh apples, pears, and plums, along with baskets of fresh blueberries, are offered for sale. The following recipe from Zacatlán makes a good brunch dish.

Ingredients:

> 6 eggs
> 2 tablespoons finely chopped fresh parsley
> salt and pepper
> 1 large, ripe apple, unpeeled, cored and very thinly sliced into half-moons
> 4 tablespoons of butter

Beat the eggs with the parsley, salt and pepper to taste. In a large skillet, melt the butter and briefly sauté the apples, which should retain some crispness. Add the eggs and cook over low heat until the bottom is set and golden, forming a large pancake; turn and cook the other side. Transfer to a plate and cut in wedges. Serves 4.

Sopa de Habas Frescas
Fresh Fava Bean Soup

Fresh fava beans are abundant in this area during the spring months, when they are cooked fresh. They are also dried to be used during the meatless Lenten season, when they are served as one of the traditional foods of *Semana Santa*.

Ingredients:

> 1 lb. fresh fava beans
> 4 medium roma tomatoes
> 1/2 medium white onion, peeled
> 1 large clove garlic, peeled
> 2 tablespoons corn oil
> 1 1/2 quarts home made chicken or vegetable broth
> 2 tablespoons chopped cilantro
> 1-2 pasilla chiles, seeded and deveined, cut into strips, sauteed in a little oil

salt to taste

Place the beans in a medium saucepan with water to cover and boil until tender. Drain, rinse, and slide off the outer skins.

Puree the tomatoes, onion and garlic with 1/2 cup water. Heat the oil in a large saucepan, and add the tomato puree, pushing it through a strainer. Cook on medium heat, stirring occasionally, for 10 minutes. Add the beans, cilantro and broth and continue cooking for 10 minutes more. Add salt to taste. Serve hot, garnished with the sautéed pasilla chile strips. Serves 6.

Caldo de Pescado
Fish Filets in Herb and Spice Broth

The mountain streams, lakes and rivers of northern Puebla contain several varieties of fish and shellfish, including trout, perch, and river shrimp. In the following recipe, the vegetables, herbs and spices are simmered together to produce a savory broth in which the fish filets are cooked. Any kind of fish can be used, as long as it is as fresh as possible.

Ingredients:

1 1/2 lbs. fish filets, cut into 2"-thick pieces
4-5 roma tomatoes, lightly roasted
1 medium white onion, peeled and coarsely chopped
2 large garlic cloves, peeled
2 tablespoons vegetable oil
1 ancho chile, seeded, deveined and soaked in water until soft
1 tablespoon vinegar
2 whole cloves
2" piece cinnamon stick
3 black peppercorns
1 1/2 quarts water
1 sprig parsley
2 tablespoons chopped cilantro
salt to taste

Place the pieces of fish on a platter, sprinkle with salt and pepper and set aside. Puree the tomatoes, onion and garlic; heat the oil in a large saucepan or stockpot and cook the puree for 5 minutes over medium heat.

Grind the chile, vinegar and spices together in a molcajete or blender, add to the tomato puree and continue cooking another 5 minutes. Add the water, parsley, cilantro and salt to taste; bring to a boil, lower heat, cover and simmer for 30 minutes. Add fish and continue cooking until just cooked through. Serve garnished with strips of pickled jalapeños, if desired. Serves 6.

Chipotles en Conserva
Pickled Smoked Chiles

Also referred to locally by the whimsical name *chipocludos*, these chiles have a distinctive sweet-and-spicy flavor. The chipotles - dried, smoked jalapeños - are pickled in a vinegar and brown sugar solution, with garlic, herbs and spices. Most municipal markets in the region have a row of women who sit behind huge *cazuelas*, ladling out a variety of pickled chiles into plastic bags, which the customer will either take home or use to accompany tacos, tortas, or other foods sold in the market. This recipe comes from Estela Salas Silva, of the Mexican Home Cooking school, and was passed on to her by her grandmother, a traditional Puebla cook. These chiles are particularly good served with grilled meat and beans.

Ingredients:

>10 dried chipotle chiles
>10 dried morita chiles
>4 whole heads garlic, tips removed
>1 1/2 large white onions, sliced into thin rings
>2 cones *piloncillo* or two cups firmly packed dark brown sugar
>1/2 cup vinegar
>1/4 cup olive oil

4-5 bay leaves
3-4 sprigs thyme
salt to taste.

Bring 1 1/2 quarts of water to a boil, add chiles and whole garlic bulbs and simmer, partially covered, until the chiles are soft, about 1 hour.

Add remaining ingredients, using more vinegar if desired, to cut down on the heat, which the vinegar absorbs. Continue cooking for another 1/2 hour.

Let sit uncovered overnight, transfer to jars and refrigerate. Makes 2 quarts.

Chiles en Escabeche
Pickled Chiles with Vegetables

Fresh green chiles are pickled with carrots, onions, herbs and spices and either sold right from the *cazuelas* or packed into glass jars, in which they make a very attractive, multi-colored presentation. Serranos, jalapeños or the very large jalapeños known as *huachinangos* in Puebla can be used. Packed into sterile glass jars and sealed, these make a nice gift, as do the pickled chipotles, above.

Ingredients:

2 lb. carrots, cut in thin rounds
3 lb. pearl onions, peeled
1 1/2 lb. whole fresh serrano or jalapeño chiles
3 whole heads garlic, separated into individual cloves and peeled
10 bay leaves
1/2 teaspoon whole black peppercorns
1 1/2 tablespoons dried oregano leaves
6 sprigs thyme
6 sprigs marjoram
1 tablespoon salt
1 quart white vinegar

2 cups water
3/4 cup olive oil

Combine vegetables and spices in a 2-quart glass jar. Bring the vinegar and water to a boil and remove from heat; stir in olive oil. Pour pickling solution over ingredients in jar, mix well and marinate 4-5 days before transferring to the refrigerator for longer storage. Makes 2 quarts.

Pescado en Pipian Rojo
Fish in Red Pipian

While a green pipian nearly always contains pumpkin seeds, the red version features sesame seeds, either alone or in combination with other seeds. While typically found all over the state of Puebla, *pipian rojo* is normally associated with chicken. This version, using fish, originated in the *sierra.*

Ingredients:

For the fish:

2 quarts water
2 lbs. firm white fish fillets
1 medium white onion, peeled and cut in half
2 bay leaves
1 sprig thyme
salt to taste

For the sauce:

6 tablespoons sesame seeds, lightly toasted
3-6 tablespoons ancho chile seeds, according to the degree of heat desired
2 whole cloves
1 sick cinnamon, or 1/2 teaspoon ground
3 cloves garlic, roasted with skins on, then peeled
2 tablespoons corn oil, divided

1 cup hulled pumpkin seeds
4 ancho chiles, seeded, deveined and soaked in warm water
until soft
salt to taste

Bring the water to boil in a stockpot with the onions, bay
leaves, thyme and salt to taste. Add fish and simmer until just
tender. Strain and reserve broth.

Grind the sesame seeds, chile seeds, cloves, cinnamon and
roasted garlic in a molcajete or spice mill. Heat one tablespoon of
the oil and sauté the pumpkin seeds in it just until they begin to
pop. Remove from heat and puree with the ground spices, chiles,
and enough of their soaking liquid to make a paste.

Heat the remaining tablespoon of oil in a large saucepan,
add the paste and cook over medium heat, stirring constantly to
prevent sticking or scorching, for 5 minutes. Add the reserved fish
broth a little at a time, stirring constantly. Cook over medium heat,
stirring from time to time, until the sauce thickens. Add fish filets,
heat through, and serve the filets and sauce garnished with toasted,
coarsely ground pumpkin seeds. Serves 6.

Acamayas al Mojo de Ajo
Shellfish in Garlic Sauce

The town of Tenampulco sits in a tropical mountain valley
in the far northeastern part of the state of Puebla, bordering on
Veracruz. Surrounded by rivers, waterfalls and hot springs, this is
a paradise for fresh fish and shellfish lovers. *Acamayas,* the large
river crawfish that abound here, are taken from the water and
grilled over hot coals right on the shore. There are camping spots
on the Apulco River where one can swim, fish, go boating, and
enjoy these delicacies prepared to order by the local women.
Jumbo shrimp can be substituted for the *acamayas* in this recipe.

Ingredients:

1/2 cup butter
1/2 cup olive oil

4 large cloves garlic, peeled and finely chopped
2 canned chipotle chiles in adobo sauce, chopped
12 large crawfish or jumbo shrimp
Salt and pepper to taste

In a large skillet, heat the butter and olive oil over medium heat. Add the garlic and cook until soft, taking care not to overcook or brown; stir in the chipotles.

Add the crawfish or shrimp and cook for 10 minutes, or until done. If you are using shrimp, they will require less cooking time. Taste for salt and pepper; serve immediately. Serves 4.

Mixiotes
Spiced Meat Steamed in Parchment

The word *mixiote* refers both to the bundle of spiced meat and to the wrapper in which it was traditionally steamed, the outermost layer of the *maguey* leaf, called a *penca*. (*Maguey* is the century plant, a succulent from which the ancient beverage *pulque* is derived. So valuable was this plant to the people of this region that one legend has it that the god-prince Quetzalcoatl sent shooting stars to earth to form the first *maguey* plants.) This thin outer leaf layer is similar to parchment paper in thickness and consistency. Today, *papel para mixiotes*, a textured paper, is a commonly used substitute for the endangered *pencas.*

One of the most characteristic dishes of the *sierra*, these succulent bundles are made with a variety of meat, including lamb, beef, and chicken. They often, but not always, contain carrots and potatoes. They may be made in quantity and frozen for later use.

Ingredients:

12 chicken thighs, or 3 1/2 lbs. of lamb or beef cubes
1 cup bitter (Seville) orange juice, or 1/2 cup sweet orange juice and 1/2 cup white vinegar
1/2 head garlic, peeled and chopped
1/4 teaspoon each dried marjoram, dried thyme dried oregano

2 bay leaves

6 ancho chiles, seeded and deveined, soaked in warm water until soft

6 guajillo chiles, seeded and deveined, soaked in warm water until soft

3 1/2 cups water

1 medium white onion, peeled and chopped

2 roma tomatoes, roasted and peeled

12 small new potatoes, cut in 1" cubes

6 medium carrots, sliced

12 dried avocado leaves

6 *mixiotes*, cut in half, or 12 pieces of mixiote paper or 8"x8" pieces of double-thickness parchment paper

Salt and pepper the chicken thighs or meat cubes and prick them in several places with a fork. Puree the Seville orange juice with the garlic and spices and pour this mixture into a large bowl. Place the chicken or meat in this marinade and set them aside while the sauce is prepared.

Puree the chiles with the onion, tomato and salt to taste. Strain the puree into a medium saucepan and simmer for about 10 minutes.

Place an avocado leaf, a piece of chicken or a few meat cubes, a few potatoes and carrots, and a few spoonfuls of tomato sauce into each *mixiote* or paper square. Tie each package with twine or string.

Put water in a large stockpot or steamer with a rack and place the mixiotes on the rack. Cover tightly and steam 1 1/2 to 2 hours. To serve, place each mixiote in a soup bowl. Each diner unties and unwraps his own mixiote, letting the liquid flow into the bowl with the meat and vegetables. Serve with sliced avocado, warm tortillas and green salsa. Serves 12

Pollo Encacahuatado
Chicken in Peanut Sauce

The town of Huauchinango, set in a lovely cloud forest where a variety of plants abound, is famous for its good cooking and many small family restaurants, where this dish is one of the local specialties. *Cacahuate*, the melodic word for peanut, comes from the Nahuatl *tlal-cacahuatl*, meaning earth-cocoa, because of the plant's peculiar habit of sending flowers upward, only to droop over into the ground, where the fruit develops. The flower apparently falls quickly, because for several years, the Spaniards were puzzled as to how the flower and the fruit could be in two different places.

Ingredients:

1 whole chicken, cut into serving pieces
4 tablespoons lard or corn oil, divided
2 roma tomatoes, roasted and peeled
1/2 medium white onion, peeled and chopped
1 large garlic clove, peeled
1/2 cup shelled peanuts, skins removed
1 ancho chile, seeded, deveined and soaked in warm water until soft
1 stick cinnamon
1 teaspoon dark brown sugar
2 cups chicken broth
salt to taste

Season the chicken with salt and pepper; sauté it in a large skillet until golden. While the chicken is browning, make the sauce.

Puree the tomatoes, onion and garlic, with a little water, until smooth. Heat the remaining 2 tablespoons of lard or oil in a large saucepan, add the tomato puree and cook over medium heat for 5 minutes. Liquefy the peanuts, chile, cinnamon, and sugar with the chicken broth. Add this mixture to the tomato puree and cook the sauce for another 5 minutes.

Transfer the browned chicken to the pan containing the sauce, cover and cook on low heat for 35-40 minutes, checking the pieces of white meat for doneness first. Serve in shallow bowls, with some sauce spooned over and under each piece of chicken. Serves 6.

Lentejas con Carne de Puerco
Lentils with Pork

The use of legumes in many guises is characteristic of this region. Faithful to the customs of their ancestors, the people of Tepeyahualco, in the eastern *sierra*, eat one form of them or another every day. Their lentil and pork stew is particularly satisfying in chilly weather. It benefits from next-day reheating, after the lentils have absorbed the full flavor.

Ingredients:

> 2 tablespoons lard or corn oil
> 1 lb. pork stew meat, cut in 1" cubes
> 1/2 medium white onion, chopped
> 2 large garlic cloves, chopped
> 1/2 lb. tomatillos, husked
> 1-2 canned chipotle chiles in adobo sauce
> 1/2 teaspoon ground cumin
> 1/4 teaspoon freshly ground black pepper
> 1/4 teaspoon dried oregano leaves
> 1/2 teaspoon cinnamon
> 2 cups dried lentils
> 4 cups water
> salt to taste

Heat the lard or oil in a large, heavy-bottomed saucepan or *cazuela*, add the meat and sauté until brown on the outside. Add the onion and garlic and continue to sauté, over medium heat, until the onion begins to get soft. Boil the tomatillos in water to cover, drain and puree with the chipotles. Add the puree to the pork and vegetables, along with the rest of the ingredients. Bring to a boil, lower heat and simmer until the lentils are tender, adding boiling water if necessary. Serve in shallow bowls, with a garnish of chopped cilantro if desired. Serves 6.

Conserva de Manzana y Ciruela
Apple and Plum Preserves

Glasses of preserves, conserves and marmalades from the *sierra* are stacked in booths at nearly every autumn fair in Puebla. This recipe and the following are typical of the area, where one fruit is quite often preserved in combination with another.

Ingredients:

    5 large green apples, peeled, cored and cubed
    5 lbs. plums, halved and pitted
    8 cups sugar
    rind and juice of 2 oranges
    1 stick cinnamon

Place the apples and plums in a large, stainless steel or glass bowl and toss with sugar; let stand at room temperature 8 hours. Sliver the orange rind and place it in a heavy-bottomed saucepan with the juice, fruit and cinnamon. Cook over low heat, stirring occasionally, until the conserve thickens and the fruit is translucent, about 45 minutes. Ladle into sterile jars and seal. Makes about 10 jelly glasses.

Mermelada de Pera y Chabacano
Pear and Apricot Marmelade

Ingredients:

    3 lb. firm pears, peeled and cored
    3 lb. apricots, halved and pitted
    1 orange
    4-5 cups sugar
    1 stick cinnamon
    1 vanilla bean

Put the fruit through a grinder, or use a food processor, to chop coarsely. Place the fruit, along with any juices extracted during the chopping, in a heavy-bottomed saucepan with the sugar, cinnamon and vanilla. Simmer for 45 minutes or until mixture thickens, stirring occasionally to keep the marmalade from sticking. Remove the cinnamon stick and vanilla bean; ladle into sterile jars and seal. Makes about 4 quarts.

Atole de Mora
Blackberry Atole

Berries of all kinds grow throughout the *sierra* and, in addition to being made into   jams and preserves, are used to flavor *atole*, the corn-based drink served hot as an early morning and late evening drink, most often with tamales. This blackberry *atole* is a specialty of Huauchinango, Puebla. Other varieties of fresh berries or other fruit (such as peaches, mangos and guavas) may be used, with the amount of sugar adjusted according to the sweetness of the fruit.

Ingredients:

> 1/2 cup fresh masa or 1/2 cup masa harina mixed with 1/4 cup water until smooth
> 5 cups water
> 1 cup light cream or half and half
> 1/4 cup ground piloncillo or dark brown sugar
> 1/2 teaspoon vanilla extract
> 1 cup blackberries or other fruit, mashed and strained

In a heavy-bottomed saucepan, dissolve the masa in water and cook over low heat, stirring, until the mixture begins to thicken. Add the milk gradually, still stirring, followed by the sugar.
When the sugar has dissolved, remove the mixture from the heat and stir in the vanilla extract and fruit. Serve hot in mugs. Serves 6.

Café de Olla
Sweet Cinnamon Coffee

The annual Cuetzalan Coffee Festival, held every October, attracts visitors from all over Mexico to the *Sierra de Puebla* to buy freshly roasted coffee beans and unique handcrafts such as the clay stoves, shaped like dogs, which hold clay comals for baking tortillas and *cazuelas* for cooking stews.

The celebration, which lasts for a week, includes dancers from the local villages and *voladores*, or "flyers", who perform a Totonac ritual which involves spinning from a 50-to-100 foot high pole set into the ground, which has been blessed with offerings. People stay up until the pre-dawn hours, kept warm by this sweet coffee, which is traditionally served late at night throughout Mexico.

Ingredients:

> 6 cups water
> 3 heaping tablespoons medium-grind coffee (not instant)
> 1 stick cinnamon
> 4 tablespoons brown sugar or ground *piloncillo*, or to taste

Bring the water to boil in a medium saucepan, add the coffee, cinnamon and sugar and continue boiling for 30 seconds. Stir and strain into mugs. Makes 6 servings.

Copacabana
Rum and Coffee After Dinner Drink

Cuetzalan's *cafe de altura*, mountain grown coffee, goes perfectly with Mexican dark rum and vanilla ice cream. This is a dessert and after dinner drink in one.

Ingredients:

    1 square semi-sweet chocolate
    4 oucnes freshly brewed coffee
    1 1/2 ounces dark rum
    1 scoop vanilla ice cream

Place the chocolate at the bottom of a parfait glass. Add the rum. Pour the hot coffee into the glass and add a scoop of vanilla ice cream. Serve immediately.

molinillo
y
chocolate

CHAPTER V

La Mixteca Poblana:
Puebla's Southern Cooking

The southern part of the state, known as the *Mixteca Poblana*, is really the ancient corn belt, and it is said there that corn "was discovered as a wild god and converted to a domestic god." Tehuacan, the most important city in the region, means "the place of the gods." This region of Puebla has the oldest known history of the domestication of corn, a staple fundamental to the cuisine of Mexico and the nourishment of its people. Corn in one form or another, either as food or beverage, is consumed with nearly every meal.

The wildly beautiful *Mixteca Poblana* is a desert area filled with spectacular rock formations and so many varieties of rare cacti that parts of it have been declared biological reserves. Because of this rugged terrain, the people of this region are often more isolated than those in other parts of the state and less exposed to elements of modern life. Cooking is still largely done in *cazuelas* or by dry-heat on a *comal*, the pre-Hispanic clay disc placed directly over the source of heat.

The *comal* is nowadays most often made of metal, but here in mostly indigenous southern Puebla, the clay version is widely used, as it is in Oaxaca, which borders the *Mixteca Poblana* and has a distinct influence on southern *poblano* cooking. Passing the huge stands of organ cactus which characterize this region, the traveler cannot tell where Puebla ends and Oaxaca begins.

The one city among the towns and villages of the region is Tehuacan, small but cosmopolitan, and well known as the center for bottling the pure delicious water from the area's many mineral springs. So numerous are they that, in Mexico, mineral water is frequently referred to as *agua de Tehuacan*. Because of these springs, there are a number of spas, called *balnearios*, on the outskirts of the city. They attract many Mexican and foreign visitors, generating a brisk hotel and restaurant trade. In recent years, some very elegant restaurants have opened in and around Tehuacan, specializing in new combinations of traditional ingredients and the creative presentation of dishes.

At the opposite end of the spectrum of dining experience are the deep-pit barbeques associated with the ancient ritual slaughtering of goats which takes place every November. In October, the goat-herding nomads of the desert start to gather at the abandoned ex-haciendas of southern Puebla to divide the work involved in making use of every part of the animal: soap from the fat, buttons and knife handles from the bone, and jerky prepared by drying the meat in the sun.

The haciendas where these gatherings take place were once the homes of the wealthy sugar plantations. The processing of sugar into rum and *aguardiente*, a strong cane alcohol, is still an important industry in the region, and many different types of fermented beverages are popular here. So, too, is sugar-coated, crystallized and candied fruit of every description. It is difficult to leave the southern part of the state without having sampled some of their exotic drinks and bought some candied fruit to take home, along with memories of the dramatic scenery and traditional lifestyle which characterize this part of the country.

Masa
Basic Corn Dough

The *tortillería*, along with the widespread availability of *masa harina* (prepared corn dough flour) has made the soaking and grinding of corn for dough less common in recent years. However, many people still do this at home, especially for special occasions.

A paste-like dough is made out of corn kernels which have previously been dried, soaked in a solution of water and powdered lime, and simmered until the skins can be removed by rubbing the kernels between the palms of the hands. The kernels need to sit in their simmering solution for about a day until the skin, as well as the "eye" at the base of each kernel, can be removed and the grinding begin.

This procedure is quite time-consuming, and the right kind of dried corn kernels infrequently found outside Mexico. Packaged *masa harina*, however, is easy to find and makes very acceptable masa. Quaker, Maseca and White Feather brands are all widely available north of the border. For those interested in preparing the dough from dried corn kernels- a large-kernelled variety resembling hominy is required- an excellent, detailed description of the step by step process is given in Diana Kennedy's *The Tortilla Book.* A well-seasoned or non-stick griddle is a fine substitute for a comal.

Ingredients:

> For 1 lb. *masa*:

> 2 1/4 cups dry *masa harina* (Quaker, Maseca, etc.)
> 1/2 teaspoon salt
> 1 1/2 cups warm water

Combine the ingredients in a bowl, then turn the dough out to need on a flat surface. It will have a sticky consistency at first, but will become smooth and pliable as you knead. This will take about 5 minutes. After kneading, let the dough rest another 5 minutes before shaping and cooking on a griddle or *comal.* This recipe makes enough dough for 12 medium tortillas, 12 *molotes* (Chapter IV) or 24 *chalupas* (Chapter II.)

Tortillas Caseras
Homemade Tortillas

Even the smallest towns in Mexico have at least one *tortillería* dispensing fresh hot tortillas daily. The location of a *tortillería* is unfailingly indicated by the line that forms outside every mid-afternoon at the hour of *comida*, the multi-course main meal of the day.

Although fresh tortillas can be purchased anywhere in Mexico, the same is not true for its northern neighbor.

Homemade tortillas are worth the little bit of effort, therefore, if you are serving an authentic Mexican meal. You will need a tortilla press, an inexpensive item widely available in the US in Hispanic markets and kitchen supply stores. Although some are made of wood, most tortilla presses consist of two metal plates, held together by a hinge, with a lever that presses the two plates together to flatten a ball of dough into a tortilla. You will also need squares of waxed paper, cut to fit the dimensions of the tortilla press, to keep the dough from sticking.

Ingredients:

> 1 recipe Basic Corn Dough (above)
> Warm water, as necessary

After the dough has been kneaded until smooth and non-sticky, heat a well-seasoned or nonstick griddle, or a comal, until a drop of water sprinkled on the surface evaporates. Pinch off a 1 1/2"-2" piece of dough for each tortilla. Place the dough between the waxed paper squares lining the tortilla press, and push down on the lever, flattening the dough. Carefully remove each tortilla by peeling it away from the waxed paper. If the tortilla has cracked around the edges while being pressed, the dough is probably too dry and a little water will have to be added and kneaded in.

Toss the tortilla back and forth from one flattened palm of your hand to the other a few times to aerate it. Place it on the hot griddle or comal and bake it for 30 seconds; turn it over and bake 1 minute. Turn it over again and bake another 30 seconds. Dark spots on the tortilla indicate that the surface of the griddle or comal is too hot.

Although tortillas are baked on a dry surface, you may need to rub it with a small amount of vegetable oil, applied with a paper towel, if the tortilla sticks. A griddle or comal reserved solely for tortilla making will season nicely after the first few uses and will not need to be oiled. As the tortillas are removed from the heat, they should be stacked inside a cloth and, at serving time, brought to the table in the cloth or tucked inside a covered basket. Makes 12.

Chiltamales
Chiles Stuffed with Fresh Corn Tamales

Unlike most tamales, which are made from a dough that starts out as dried corn kernels or flour made from them, these tamales are made from corn cut fresh from the cob. The dough is tucked into poblano chiles and steamed in the fresh husks. In southern Puebla, they are usually made with red poblanos, in season in late summer. Although the corn kernels would traditionally be mashed on a *metate*, using a blender or food processor makes this recipe an easy one.

Ingredients:

    4 cups corn kernels, cut fresh from the cob
    1/4 cup milk
    2 tablespoons cornstarch
    1/2 cup unsalted butter, melted
    1/4 cup sugar
    1 teaspoon salt
    8 fresh red or green poblano chiles, roasted and peeled
    16 fresh corn husks

Liquefy the corn with the milk in a blender or food processor until a fine puree is obtained. Scrape the puree into a mixing bowl and add the cornstarch, butter, sugar and salt, beating well after each addition. Cut a lengthwise slit up the side of each chile and carefully remove the seed sac. Divide the corn mixture evenly among the chiles, filling them loosely to allow for expansion as the batter steams. Wrap each chile in two corn husks, and then in a double thickness of parchment paper. Place them on a rack in a stockpot or steamer with water in the bottom. Cover and steam for 1 hour. Remove the paper and husks and serve the *chiltamales* hot, with a dusting of crumbled hard cheese if desired, and salsa and Mexican *crema* on the side. Makes 8.

Envueltos de Mole
Chicken and Fruit Stuffed Enchiladas

Envueltos means "wrapped", in this case referring to tortillas wrapped around a savory filling. These enchiladas are bathed in a simple mole sauce which is typically hotter than those found in other parts of the state. Another distinctly southern aspect of this dish is the presence of plantains in the filling.

Ingredients:

For the *envueltos*:

1 chicken breast, poached, skinned, boned and shredded, broth reserved
1 tablespoon lard or corn oil
1/2 large white onion, peeled and chopped
1 plantain, peeled and chopped
1 apple, peeled, cored and chopped
1 tablespoon raisins
1 tablespoon almonds
2 roma tomatoes, roasted, peeled, seeded and finely chopped
1/4 cup chopped fresh parsley
salt and pepper to taste
16 medium corn tortillas

For the *mole* sauce:

4 tablespoons lard or corn oil
2 tablespoons sugar
1/2 lb. mulato chiles, seeded and soaked in warm water until soft
2 1/2 ounces chipotle chiles, seeded and soaked in water until soft

1 lb. roma tomatoes, roasted and peeled
1 plantain, peeled and sliced
1/2 cinnamon stick
1 small corn tortilla, torn in pieces
1 ounce Mexican chocolate (1/2 tablet)

To make the filling, heat the lard or oil in a large skillet and sauté the onion over medium heat until it starts to soften. Add the plantain, apple, raisins, almonds and tomatoes and cook for another 5 minutes. Add the chicken and parsley and cook just until heated through. Add salt and pepper to taste.

To make the sauce, heat half of the lard or oil in a heavy saucepan. Add the sugar and cook, stirring over low heat just until the sugar begins to caramelize. Carefully add the soaked chiles and continue cooking for another minute. Transfer to a blender, add the tomatoes, and puree until smooth.

Heat another tablespoon of the lard or oil and add the plantain, cinnamon, tortilla and chocolate; cook, stirring constantly, until the chocolate melts. Add this mixture to the puree in the blender and liquefy, adding reserved broth as necessary to achieve a smooth paste. This may be done in two batches. Transfer to a large, heavy bottomed saucepan or *cazuela* in which the remaining tablespoon of lard or oil has been heated. Gradually add broth, stirring constantly, until the mole reaches the desired consistency. Cook for 30 minutes on low heat, stirring frequently to prevent scorching, adding broth as necessary.

To assemble the *envueltos*, pass each tortilla through the sauce until it is coated. (If the tortillas are packaged rather than fresh, you will have to soften them first by soft-frying in a bit of oil until they are pliable.) Place some of the filling down the center of each tortilla and fold both sides over the center. Serve immediately, garnished with thinly sliced onion rings and crumbled *queso añejo* or other hard cheese if desired. Serves 8.

Crema de Frijol
Pureed Black Bean Soup

One of our favorite relaxing getaways is the Casa Cantarranas, a lovely hotel in Tehuacan built on the site of the old Hotel Peñafiel, an elegant turn-of-the-century spa. One can still visualize well-dressed ladies, carefully shielded from the sun by parasols, strolling the grounds with distinguished Porfirian gentlemen. One thing they didn't have, though, was Mexican nouvelle cuisine, combining the traditional ingredients with modern presentation, which is a specialty of Casa Cantarranas' kitchen. The soups are beautifully garnished with swirls of *crema*, forming a design with the tines of a fork.

Ingredients:

> 6 ounces dried black beans
> 1 large white onion, peeled and cut in quarters
> 3 large garlic cloves, peeled
> 1 sprig epazote
> 2 tablespoons lard or oil
> 2 roma tomatoes
> 1/4 teaspoon dried oregano leaves
> salt to taste
> Mexican crema or crème fraîche, for garnish

Soak the beans in a large pot with water to cover overnight; add 3/4 of the onion, 2 cloves of the garlic, the epazote and 1 tablespoon of the lard or oil. Bring to a boil, lower heat and simmer, covered, until the beans are tender.

Puree the beans, with their broth, in a blender or food processor until smooth. Taste for salt. Strain through a wide mesh strainer, pushing through as much as possible with a spoon, and set aside.

Puree the tomatoes with the remaining 1/4 onion, the remaining garlic clove and the oregano. Heat the remaining tablespoon of lard or oil in a large heavy-bottomed pot or cazuela. Sauté the tomato puree 10 minutes, add the bean puree and cook until the soup comes to a boil. Serve hot in bowls, garnished with crema. Serves 6.

Sopa de Ajo
Garlic Soup

San Gabriel Chilac, the southern Puebla town famous for hand-embroidered blouses and dresses, is a garlic-growing region providing this indispensable culinary ingredient to much of the area, where this soup is served with the piquant addition of arbol chile.

Ingredients:

1 head garlic, peeled and thinly sliced
2 tablespoons butter
2 tablespoons olive oil
1 arbol chile, soaked in hot water for 25 minutes (seeded, if desired)
2 roma tomatoes, roasted and peeled
1 quart hot chicken, beef or vegetable stock
salt to taste
4 eggs
1/2 baguette, cut in 1/4" rounds and sautéed in butter until golden
2 tablespoons crumbled *queso fresco* or feta cheese
2 tablespoons chopped fresh parsley

In a large saucepan over medium heat, sauté the garlic until golden in the butter and oil. Puree the chile and tomatoes and add to the garlic.

Continue cooking until thick, add the stock and bring to a boil. Add salt to taste. Break each egg into a dish and slide into the boiling broth. When the eggs are poached, place each in a serving bowl with the soup, baguette rounds, and a sprinkling of cheese and parsley. Serves 4.

Arroz a la Mexicana
Mexican Red Rice

Served all over the country, this rice is generally associated with Puebla because it is the traditional side dish with *mole poblano*. In the southern part of the state, it accompanies *envueltos de mole* (this chapter.)

Ingredients:

> 1 cup long-grain rice
> 2 tablespoons lard or corn oil
> 2 roma tomatoes, roasted and peeled
> 1/2 small white onion, chopped
> 2 cloves garlic, peeled
> 1/4 cup each diced carrots and potatoes
> 1/2 cup fresh or frozen peas
> 2 1/2 cups hot chicken broth
> salt to taste

Soak the rice in hot water to cover for 15 minutes, rinse in a strainer or colander under cold water until the water runs clear. Allow to dry before cooking.

Heat the lard or oil in a heavy-bottomed pot or cazuela and sauté the rice until golden.

Liquefy the tomatoes, onion and garlic with 1/2 cup of the broth, add to rice and cook over medium flame until the liquid is absorbed. Stir in the vegetables, add remaining broth, cover and simmer until all liquid is absorbed. Let sit for a few minutes, stir to combine vegetables and rice, and taste for salt. Serves 6.

Pollo en Amaranto
Chicken in Amaranth Sauce

In Tehuacan's main plaza, there is a kiosk set up to distribute information on the amaranth plant, long cultivated here for its seeds, which the pre-Hispanic people valued so highly for their nutritive properties that they shaped them into idols.

Today amaranth is most commonly found in the bars of homemade candy called *alegrías*, sold in plazas throughout Mexico. The tiny dried amaranth seeds used in this recipe are found in health food stores everywhere. The Greeks, who called them *amarantos*, meaning "not fading", believed that they contained life-prolonging properties.

Ingredients:

> 4 lbs. chicken pieces (breast halves, thighs or a combination)
> 2 tablespoons corn oil
> 2 1/2 cups amaranth seeds, lightly toasted in a dry skillet
> 1 lb. tomatoes, roasted and charred
> 2 canned chipotle chiles in adobo sauce
> 3 large garlic cloves, peeled and chopped
> 1/4 cup chopped onion
> 1 whole clove
> 1/2 teaspoon whole black peppercorns
> 2" piece cinnamon stick
> 4 guajillo chiles, seeded and soaked 25 minutes in hot water to soften
> 3 1/2 cups chicken broth
> 3/4 lb. potatoes, boiled, peeled and cut into cubes
> salt to taste

In a large pot or Dutch oven, sauté the chicken lightly in just enough oil to prevent sticking; add water to cover, with salt to taste. Cook until chicken is tender, set chicken aside and strain the broth.

In a blender or food processor, puree the amaranth, tomatoes, chipotles, garlic, onion, clove, peppercorns, cinnamon, drained guajillo chiles and chicken broth until smooth. This may be done in two batches.

Heat the remaining oil in a large, heavy-bottom pot or *cazuela*, add the sauce and cook over low heat for 25 minutes, stirring frequently to prevent sticking. Add the cooked chicken pieces, potatoes and salt to taste. Serve in shallow bowls, accompanied by warm corn tortillas. Serves 6-8.

Mole Verde de Hierbas
Herbed Green Mole

Green mole is most commonly found in the states of Puebla, Tlaxcala and Oaxaca. This recipe from southern Puebla reflects the influence of Oaxacan cooking, with its use of several fresh herbs, which give it an attractive bright green color. Criollo avocado leaves may be substituted for *hoja santa*. Serves 6

Ingredients:

> 2 lbs. pork stew meat, cut into 1 1/2" cubes OR 1 chicken, cut in serving pieces
> 1 large white onion, peeled and cut into wedges
> 10 large cloves garlic, peeled and cut in half
> 1 lb. tomatillos, husked
> 4 whole serrano chiles
> 2 tablespoons lard or corn oil
> 1/2 cup each chopped fresh parsley, cilantro, hoja santa and epazote
> 1 lb. tiny new potatoes, cooked until just tender
> salt to taste

Place the stew meat or chicken in a stockpot with half the onion wedges, 4 cloves garlic, water to cover and salt to taste. Bring to a boil, cover, and simmer until just tender, 35-45 minutes.

Meanwhile, place the tomatillos in a large saucepan with the remaining onion wedges, 4 more of the garlic cloves, the chiles, salt to taste and water to cover. Bring to a boil and simmer, covered, until the tomatillos are tender. Allow to cool a bit, transfer to a blender and puree.

Heat the lard or oil in a saucepan, add the tomatillo mixture and simmer about 30 minutes. Add to the pork or chicken stew, along with the potatoes. At this point, the stew may be thickened with a little masa harina mixed with water.

Using a molcajete, mortar or food processor, grind the chopped herbs with the 2 remaining cloves of garlic and salt to taste. Add this paste to the stew, stir and serve immediately. Serv

Barbacoa de Puerco
Pork Cooked in Avocado Leaves

The word *barbacoa* does not refer to barbeque as it is known north of the border, but to meat wrapped in leaves and cooked in its own juices, usually in a pit dug in the ground. Zapotitlán, in the far southeastern part of the state, is known for its *barbacoa*, as well as for its biosphere reserve containing fifty-three species of cactus not found elsewhere.

This is the place where the annual autumn goat slaughter, *la matanza*, originated. Although goat is the most common meat for *barbacoa*, the juicier and less stringy pork is a good choice. This recipe calls for the meat to be cooked in a steamer rather than a pit in the ground, but we have done it both ways. My husband once dug a pit and cooked a whole pig, wrapped in banana leaves, for fourteen hours, at which point the meat was the most tender I have ever tasted. We recently tried it with a sheep wrapped in maguey leaves with equally successful results.

Ingredients:

> 3 lbs. boneless pork leg meat, cut in cubes
> 2 cups white vinegar
> salt and pepper
> approximately 20 *criollo* avocado leaves
> 6 tablespoons melted lard or corn oil

Place the meat in a glass bowl and marinate it overnight in the vinegar, salt and pepper to taste. On the rack of a steamer or stockpot, arrange a bed of avocado leaves, then a layer of meat, alternating layers of meat and leaves. Pour the melted lard or oil over the top layer of meat and cover it with a layer of leaves. Steam 2 hours, or until meat is tender, taking care to add boiling water to replace any that has evaporated from the bottom of the steamer. Serve meat with warm tortillas and a selection of salsas. Serves 10.

Mole de Olla
Beef Stew with Vegetables

Mole de olla is found in most parts of central Mexico in one version or another. In southern Puebla, it is usually made without the addition of tomatillos used elsewhere, but relies on chiles alone for seasoning. Unlike most moles, this is not made by combining broth with a thick paste, but is actually a stew.

Ingredients:

> 2 1/2 lbs. beef shanks, bone in
> 2 quarts water
> 1 medium white onion, peeled and cut in wedges
> 1 sprig epazote
> 3 large cloves garlic
> salt to taste
> 3 tender ears of corn, cut in fourths
> 3 carrots, cut in chunks
> 1/2 lb. green beans
> 3 zucchini squash, cut in chunks
> 3 ancho chiles, seeded and soaked in hot water for 15 minutes
> 3 pasilla chiles, seeded and soaked in hot water for 15 minutes
> 2 tablespoons corn oil

Place the meat, water, 3/4 of the onion, 2 cloves of the garlic, the epazote, the corn and salt to taste in a stockpot or large *cazuela*, bring to a boil and simmer for about 2 hours, or until the meat is tender. Remove meat and corn and set aside; strain and reserve broth. Cook the carrots, green beans and zucchini separately; strain and reserve.

Grind the chiles with the remaining onion, garlic and

enough broth to just cover in a blender or food processor. In a large pot or *cazuela*, heat the oil, add the chile mixture and cook over medium heat until thickened. Add the beef broth and continue cooking for 20 minutes. Add the meat and the corn and heat through. Add the carrots, beans and zucchini and serve in bowls, accompanied by chopped onion and lemon wedges. Serves 6.

Calabaza en Tacha
Candied Pumpkin

The town of Izucar de Matamoros is famous for sugar, both refined and unrefined. The latter, called *piloncillo*, is dark brown in color and is sold in cones. It is used to sweeten everything from coffee to candied fruit. The following recipe is prepared around Day of the Dead, when the dark green Mexican pumpkins are in season, and left on the altars as an offering. It is possible that in pre-Hispanic times it was prepared with honey or boiled plant saps, but it is not clear whether conserving fruit in sweet syrup was a technique brought by the Spaniards, who had learned it from the Arabs, or whether it was actually done before their arrival.

Ingredients:

1 4 lb. pumpkin, or 2 winter squash
2 lbs. piloncillo cones or 14 cups dark brown sugar
6 cinnamon sticks
juice of 1 orange
4 cups water
1 teaspoon whole cloves, tied in cheese cloth

Poke holes, about the diameter of drinking straws, though the pumpkin in several places. In a large heavy-bottomed stockpot, place the sugar, cinnamon, orange juice, water and cloves; cook, stirring frequently, until the piloncillo has melted and the syrup has the consistency of molasses.

Add the pumpkin, using a wooden spoon to baste it with the syrup. Cook over low heat, basting frequently, until the pumpkin is tender, about 2 hours. Using 2 smaller pumpkins or winter squash will require less time. Allow the pumpkin to cool in its syrup before serving. Serve, cut up, in bowls with ice cold milk. Serves 10-12.

Bebida de Piña
Fresh Pineapple Drink

Pineapple is a very popular fruit in this part of the state, sometimes fermented into an alcoholic drink called *tepache*, and also used as a fresh mixer for rum, tequila or cane alcohol. The following drink is refreshing without the addition of any alcohol, and is often sold at street stands. With alcohol, it is popular at regional *ferias*, or fairs. The pineapple shell makes an attractive serving container.

Ingredients:

   1 fresh, sweet pineapple
   juice of 1 fresh lime
   freshly squeezed orange juice, as necessary
   rum or tequila to taste (optional)

Cut the top off the pineapple and scoop out the pulp. Push the pulp through a wide mesh strainer, obtaining as much juice as possible. Pour the juice into the pineapple shell, add the lime juice and enough orange juice to fill the shell nearly to the top. Leave room for the rum or tequilla if desired; stir and add straws. Serves 2.

Chocolate Mexicano
Mexican Chocolate Beverage

The southern towns of Tapanala and Ixcaquixtla are both known for their chocolate drinks. This is due in part to their proximity to Oaxaca, which has an old and highly regarded chocolate-making tradition. The Aztecs were fond of chocolate, not just for its caffeine but because of its versatility. It could be served as a sweet drink, flavored with honey and vanilla, or a spicy one, with the addition of chiles. The beans were fermented, cured, toasted and ground before being mixed with water to make a beverage. This is commonly whipped to a froth with a grooved wooden beater called a *molinillo*, but pre-Hispanic drawings show the froth being obtained by pouring the chocolate back and forth from one vessel to another. Nowadays Mexican chocolate is flavored with ground nuts and cinnamon and is sold packaged in pancake-like tablets.

    3-4 tablets Mexican chocolate
    6 cups water or milk
    6 cinnamon sticks

Melt the chocolate in a medium saucepan with just enough water to make a paste. Add the 6 cups water or milk; bring to a boil, stirring constantly. A *molinillo* or wire whip may be used to obtain a froth, if desired. Serve hot in mugs, with a cinnamon stick in each. Serves 6.

Index of Recipes by Course

Antojitos: Appetizers/Snacks

Sopas: Soups

Sopa de Ajo: Garlic Soup **115**

Platos Fuertes: Main Courses

Tinga Poblana: Spiced Tomato Stew **32**
Tinga Vegetariana: Vegetarian Tinga **33**
Chiles en Nogada: Stuffed Poblanos in Walnut Cream Sauce **39**
Mole del Convento de Santa Rosa: Tradicional Mole Poblano **42**
Manchamanteles Poblanos: Chicken and Fruit Stew **45**
Pipian Verde: Chicken in Pumpkin Seed Sauce **76**
Pipian Verde Vegetariano: Vegetarian Green Pipian **78**
Pollo Poblano: Chicken in Poblano Cream Sauce **78**
Pollo Atlizquense: Grilled Marinated Chicken Breasts **79**
Carne de Cerdo en Adobo: Pork in Adobo **81**
Pescado en Pipian Rojo: Fish in Red Pipian **96**
Acamayas al Mojo de Ajo: Shellfish with Garlic **97**
Mixtotes: Spiced Meat Steamed in Parchment **98**
Pollo Encacahuatado: Chicken in Peanut Sauce **99**
Lentejas con Puerco: Lentils with Pork **101**
Pollo en Amaranto: Chicken in Amaranth Sauce **116**
Mole Verde de Hierbas: Herbed Green Mole**118**
Barbacoa de Puerco: Pork Cooked in Avocado Leaves **119**
Mole de Olla: Beef Stew with Vegetables **120**

Verduras y Platos Secundarios: Vegetables and Side Dishes

Setas con Epazote: Oyster Mushrooms with Epazote **30**
Arroz Verde Poblano: Puebla Style Green Rice **38**
Champiñones al Guajillo: Mushrooms with Garlic and Chile **71**
Arroz Blanco con Verduras: White Rice with Vegetables **72**
Ensalada de Nopalitos: Nopales Salad **73**
Huaraches: Stuffed Nopales **75**
Rajas con Crema: Poblano Chile Strips with Cream **76**
Arroz a la Mexicana: Mexican Red Rice **116**

Salsas y Chiles Encurtidos: Salsas and Pickled Chiles

Salsa de Chipotle: Chipotle Chile Salsa **28**
Salsa Verde: Green Salsa **29**
Salsa Verde con Aguacate: Green Sauce with Avocado **29**
Salsa Verde Cruda: Uncooked Green Salsa **30**
Salsa de Jitomate: Roasted Tomato Salsa **89**
Chipotles en Conserva: Pickled Smoked Chiles **94**
Chiles en Escabeche: Pickled Chiles with Vegetables **95**

Postres y Dulces: Desserts and Sweets

Mousse Al Rompope: Rompope Mousse **48**
Fresas al Rompope: Strawberries with Rompope Cream **48**
Arroz con Leche: Mexican Rice Pudding **49**
Pastel de Almendras: Layered Almond Cake **50**
Cocada: Coconut Dessert **51**
Dulce de Limón: Candied Limes with Coconut Filling **52**
Camotes: Sweet Potato Candy **54**
Rosca de Reyes: Three Kings Bread **82**
Figuritas de Almendra: Almond Paste Candy **84**
Conserva de Manzana y Ciruela: Apple and Plum Preserves **102**
Mermelada de Pera y Chabacano: Pear Apricot Marmelade **102**
Calabaza en Tacha: Candied Pumpkin **121**

Bebidas: Beverages

Rompope de Santa Clara: Mexican Eggnog **47**
Champurrado: Hot ChocolateDrink **64**
Ponche Navideño: Holiday Punch **85**
Atole de Mora: Blackberry Atole **103**
Café de Olla: Sweet Cinnamon Coffee **104**
Bebida de Piña: Fresh Pineapple Drink **122**
Chocolate Mexicano: Mexican Chocolate Beverage **122**
*Copacabana:*Rum and Coffee After Dinner Drink **105**

19676600R00080

Made in the USA
San Bernardino, CA
08 March 2015